1991

SAINT THOMAS AQUINAS

ON THE UNITY OF THE INTELLECT AGAINST THE AVERROISTS

(De Unitate Intellectus Contra Averroistas)

MEDIAEVAL PHILOSOPHICAL TEXTS IN TRANSLATION

NO. 19

Marquette University Press

Milwaukee, Wisconsin

SAINT THOMAS AQUINAS

ON THE UNITY OF THE INTELLECT AGAINST THE AVERROISTS

(De Unitate Intellectus Contra Averroistas)

*Translated from the Latin
With an Introduction*

by

Beatrice H. Zedler

MARQUETTE UNIVERSITY PRESS   MILWAUKEE, WISCONSIN

1968

Library of Congress Catalogue Card Number: 68-28029
© Copyright, 1968, The Marquette University Press
Milwaukee, Wisconsin
Printed in the United States of America

To the memory of Mary Carol
through whose love of truth
error was opposed and ignorance remedied

Table of Contents

Preface

During St. Thomas' second sojourn at Paris (1268-1272), masters and scholars were discussing Averroes' views on the intellect. Even less erudite men were aware of the doctrine that there is only one intellect for the whole human race. William of Tocco, an early biographer of Thomas Aquinas, tells of a certain soldier at Paris who was unwilling to atone for his sins because, as he put it: "If the soul of the blessed Peter is saved, I shall also be saved; for if we know by one intellect, we shall share the same destiny."

Against this error that there is one intellect for all men, Thomas Aquinas wrote, continues William of Tocco, "a wonderful work *(scriptum mirabile)* in which . . . through the very words of Aristotle which Averroes misunderstood, he pulled out this error by the roots . . . so that no one who could grasp the words of Aristotle would doubt that the aforesaid error was contrary to reason." (Quoted by Mandonnet, *Siger de Brabant,* p. 103) The *scriptum mirabile* to which William of Tocco referred was the *De Unitate Intellectus contra Averroistas.*

The critical edition of the Latin text by Leo W. Keeler, S.J., was used for the English translation contained in this book. An introduction, a bibliography, and notes are included as aids to the study of the treatise.

The translator wishes to thank Dr. James H. Robb, Chairman of the Editorial Board, for his many excellent suggestions on the text of the translation. Thanks are due also to Dr. Ida Critelli, Dr. Thomas Anderson, and Dr. Peter Maxwell, who as graduate assistants, provided some valuable help in the work on the notes.

Introduction

"Angel of the Schools though he may be, St. Thomas does not speak from some abstract philosophical heaven. It is to the thirteenth century that St. Thomas gives voice. . . ."[1] The truth of these remarks is particularly evident in St. Thomas' treatise, *On the Unity of the Intellect Against the Averroists.* A polemical work, as the title suggests, it was written to answer a difficult problem of St. Thomas' time; it confronted a challenge that Greek and Arabian philosophy had offered to Christian thinkers.

A. BACKGROUND OF THE PROBLEM OF THE DE UNITATE INTELLECTUS

The source of the problem was Aristotle's *De Anima,* notably Book III, chapter 5. After observing that in nature as a whole we find two factors, a potential factor and a productive or active factor, Aristotle says that "these distinct elements must likewise be found within the soul." He then continues:

> "And in fact mind as we have described it is what it is by virtue of becoming all things, while there is another which is what it is by virtue of making all things: this is a sort of positive state like light; for in a sense light makes potential colours into actual colours.
> "Mind in this sense of it is separable, impassible, unmixed, since it is in its essential nature activity. . . .
> ". . . in the individual, potential knowledge is in time prior to actual knowledge, but in the universe as a whole it is not prior even in time. Mind is not at one time knowing and at another not. When mind is set free from its present conditions it appears as just what it is and nothing more: this alone is immortal and eternal (we do not, however, remember its former activity because while mind in this sense is impassible, mind as passive is destructible), and without it nothing thinks."[2]

That Aristotle was here distinguishing between an active intellect that makes things actually intelligible and a passive intellect that receives these intelligibles was clear, but beyond this point his meaning was not altogether clear to his readers. What did he mean by saying that mind is "separable, impassible, unmixed," "immortal and eternal"? Could an intellect with these characteristics be a power of the human soul, or was Aristotle implying that intellect is a substance that is separate and distinct from man, and one for all men?

Among the Greek commentators, Theophrastus (ca. 370-285 B.C.) and Themistius (ca. 387 A.D.) thought Aristotle meant that both active

[1] A. C. Pegis, *Saint Thomas and the Greeks,* p. 2. (Milwaukee: Marquette University Press, 1943).

[2] Aristotle, *De Anima* III, 5, 430a 10-25, tr. J. A. Smith in *Basic Works of Aristotle,* ed. R. McKeon. (New York: Random House, 1941).

and passive intellects were parts or powers of each human soul.[3] But Alexander of Aphrodisias (ca. 200 A.D.), although he placed the passive or material intellect within the individual (and perishable) human soul, held that the active intellect is a separately existing intelligence.[4] Like Alexander, some Arabian thinkers also regarded the active or agent intellect as a separate substance and one for all men.

Avicenna (980-1037) situated his doctrine of the agent intellect within the context of his theory of emanation. At the summit of his universe is a Necessary Being, who is one, incorporeal, and the source of all other beings. This Necessary Being reflects upon itself, thereby necessarily giving rise to the first effect, a pure intelligence. This effect must be one, for from one simple thing, only one can proceed. When this First Intelligence thinks of the Necessary Being, it gives rise to a Second Intelligence. When the First Intelligence thinks of itself as necessary by the First Being, it gives rise to the soul of the outermost celestial sphere; when it thinks of itself as possible in itself it gives rise to the body of this same sphere. Then, in a similar way, the Second Intelligence gives rise to a Third Intelligence and to the soul and body of the second sphere. This emanation of intelligences and spheres is halted only with the production of the sphere of the moon and the tenth or last intelligence, which is the agent intellect or Agent Intelligence.[5]

From this Agent Intelligence, which is one for all men, intelligible forms or species are infused into possible intellects belonging to individual human souls. But these souls can receive the species only after considering and comparing the images that have come from the senses. These movements prepare the soul for the "abstraction," that is, the emanation of intelligible forms.[6] But the species received by men's possible intellects are not retained. For intellectual knowledge, the soul must again be united with the separate Agent Intelligence.[7]

For Averroes (1126-1198), the famous "Commentator" on Aristotle, not only was the agent intellect a separate substance and one for all men, but also the possible intellect. Against the materialism of Alex-

[3] Theophrastus, Fragments Ia & XII in E. Barbotin, *La Théorie Aristotélicienne de l'Intellect d'après Théophraste* (Louvain: Publications Universitaires de Louvain, 1954), pp. 248-249, 270-271; Themistius, *Paraphrasis eorum quae de Anima Aristotelis*, in *Thémistius: Commentaire sur le Traité de l'Âme d'Aristote: Traduction de Guillaume de Moerbeke*, ed. G. Verbeke (Louvain: Publications Universitaires de Louvain, 1957), pp. 224-225, 235.

[4] Alexander, *De Intellectu et Intellecto*, in G. Théry, *Alexandre d'Aphrodise* (K a i n, Belgium: Le Saulchoir, 1926), pp. 74-82.

[5] Avicenna, *Metaphysica* IX, c. 4, fol. 104v-105r (Venice, 1508).

[6] Avicenna, *De Anima* V, 5, fol. 25rb-va (Venice, 1508). In the transcription by G. P. Klubertanz, S.J. (St. Louis University, 1949), pp. 125-126.

[7] *Ibid.*, V, 6, fol. 26rb-va; in Klubertanz, *op. cit.*, pp. 130-131.

ander of Aphrodisias, Averroes held that the possible or "material" intellect must be a simple, impassible substance. It cannot be "numbered to the number of individuals" but must be wholly separate from matter to insure its power for knowing universals.[8] But since this view leaves the individual man without a spiritual intellect, how then can man have intellectual knowledge?

Man's highest powers, the cogitative power, imagination, and memory, have the task of preparing the sensory data that the separate intellect will utilize. So important is this highest task that man by himself can perform, that Averroes sometimes dignifies the cogitative power with the name of intellect: not possible intellect, however, but *passible* intellect, to designate its generable and corruptible nature.[9]

The separate agent intellect makes actually intelligible the intelligible species potentially present within the phantasms provided by man's sensory powers. The separate possible intellect can then be actuated and become the subject in which knowledge exists. Men's phantasms are, for Averroes, the subject in relation to which knowledge is true.[10] Unless the data of knowledge were provided by man, the separate possible intellect would know nothing.[11] Since man as a provider of objects of knowledge, has an indispensable function in the intellect's knowing, he himself somehow shares in this knowing. Averroes is less concerned with explaining just how this can be, than with keeping the intellect free of matter to preserve its function of knowing. He had no awareness of a spiritual intellective soul that could be the form of the body without being immersed in matter.

These views of the intellect by Greek and Arabian thinkers became known to Christians of western Europe. During the twelfth and thirteenth centuries the works of Aristotle, accompanied by the commentaries of Arabian thinkers, came into Europe in Latin translation. As a result of the work of translation done at the court of Frederick II of Sicily and the School of Archbishop Raymond of Toledo, Spain, a new world of literature was introduced to Christian thinkers. Although Aristotle had previously been known and admired for his logical works, Christians now had access to other works of "The Philosopher," including his work on the soul. They were also reading in Latin translation Avicenna's *De Anima* and Averroes' *Commentary on Aristotle's De Anima.*

[8] Averroes, *Commentarium Magnum in Aristotelis de Anima Libros* III, comm. 4, pp. 383-384; comm. 5, pp. 388-389; comm. 19, p. 441; II, comm. 32, p. 178. Ed. F. S. Crawford (Cambridge, Mass.: Mediaeval Academy of America, 1953).

[9] *Ibid.*, III, comm. 6, pp. 415-416; comm. 20, pp. 449-450; comm. 33, pp. 475-476.
[10] *Ibid.*, comm. 4, pp. 384-385; comm. 5, p. 412; comm. 18, pp. 439-440.
[11] *Ibid.*, comm. 33, p. 476.

One reaction to the influx of the new literature is seen in the condemnations of 1210 and 1215. In 1210 the Provincial Council of Paris prohibited the teaching of Aristotle's works on natural philosophy or their commentaries. In 1215 the statutes of the University of Paris promulgated by Robert of Courçon, the papal legate, forbade the reading of the physical and metaphysical treatises of Aristotle and the expositions of them.[12] But the prohibitions were not effective.

Some Christians were to accept in a modified form, Avicenna's doctrine of a separate agent intellect.[13] Others were attracted by the views of Averroes. At the request of Pope Alexander IV, St. Albert wrote, in 1256, *On the Unity of the Intellect against Averroes.* Directing his treatise not against Averroes alone, but against Arabian thought, he presented thirty arguments for the unity of the human intellect and thirty-six arguments against it. He stopped with this majority of six in favor of his own position only, he said, because of lack of time.[14]

In the following decade a definite Averroist movement seemed to emerge. As more Christian thinkers read Aristotle and Averroes in Latin translation, the Philosopher was seen through the works of his Commentator. The result, for some, was that Philosophy was identified with the Commentator's positions. Philosophy itself, for these Latin Averroists, seemed to say that the possible intellect is a separate substance and one for all men. As philosophers, the Averroists held that this was the conclusion of human reason, but as Christians they refrained from saying that this doctrine was true. Without explicitly teaching a theory of "double truth," such a leading Averroist as Siger of Brabant nevertheless conveyed the impression of a conflict between faith and reason.

The Averroists' views on the intellect and their implications for Christians were censured in 1270 and 1277 in the condemnations of Etienne Tempier, Bishop of Paris.[15] They were also opposed in the writings of St. Bonaventure (1221-1274) and of Giles of Rome (ca.

12 H. Denifle and A. Chatelain (eds.), *Chartularium Universitatis Parisiensis* I (Paris, 1889) 70, 78-79.

13 Gundissalinus, *De Anima,* cap. 10, in R. de Vaux, *Notes et textes sur l'Avicennisme Latin* (Paris: Vrin, 1934), pp. 170-174; R. Bacon, *Opus Majus* I, 9; II, 5. Ed. J. H. Bridges (Oxford: Clarendon Press, 1897), Tome I, pp. 20, 38-41; H. Spettman (ed.), *Johannis Pechami Quaestiones Tractantes de Anima,* q. VI, in *Beiträge zur Geschichte der Philosophie des Mittelalters* XIX, 5-6, 73; E. Gilson, "Pourquoi saint Thomas a critiqué saint Augustin," *Archives d'Histoire Doctrinale et Littéraire du Moyen Âge* I (Paris: Vrin, 1926-1927), pp. 5-127.

14 St. Albert, *De Unitate Intellectus contra Averroem,* in *Opera Omnia,* vol. IX (Paris: Vives, 1891), pp. 437-476; F. Van Steenberghen, *Siger dans L'Histoire de l'Aristotélisme* (Louvain: Institut Supérieur de Philosophie, 1942), pp. 470-473.

15 Denifle and Chatelain (eds.), *Chartularium Universitatis Parisiensis* I, 486-487, 543-548.

1247-1316).[16] But now let us turn to St. Thomas' treatise against the Averroists.

B. The Authenticity, Date, and Title of St. Thomas' Treatise

The *De Unitate Intellectus contra Averroistas* is certainly an authentic work of St. Thomas Aquinas.[17] It was referred to in the lifetime of St. Thomas. It is found in manuscripts explicitly attributed to St. Thomas in the thirteenth century. It is listed in almost all the older catalogues of St. Thomas' writings. Its existence is presupposed by the *De Anima Intellectiva* of Siger of Brabant and by the *De Plurificatione Intellectus Possibilis* (ca. 1280) of Giles of Rome. No serious doubt has been raised about the authenticity of St. Thomas' treatise.

The *De Unitate Intellectus* is one of the later works of St. Thomas Aquinas. After his first period of teaching as a Master at Paris (1256-1259) and after his teaching at the papal curia in Italy (1259-1268), St. Thomas returned to Paris. The *De Unitate Intellectus* belongs to his second period of teaching at Paris (1268-1272). The date has been more exactly stated as the year 1270.[18] Whether the treatise was completed before or after Bishop Tempier's first condemnation of Averroism (December 10, 1270), is not definitely determined, but it is probable that the treatise was finished before the condemnation was issued.[19]

The *De Unitate Intellectus* was preceded by such works as the

[16] St. Bonaventure, *Collationes in Hexaemeron*, Sermo VI, in *Opera Omnia*, vol. IX (Paris: Vives, 1865). Giles of Rome, *Errores Philosophorum*, c. 4, #10-11, ed. J. Koch, tr. J. O. Riedl (Milwaukee: Marquette University Press, 1944); *De Plurificatione Intellectus Possibilis*, ed. F. Bocca (Rome, 1957).

[17] L. W. Keeler, S.J., Introduction to *Sancti Thomae Aquinatis Tractatus de Unitate Intellectus contra Averroistas* (Rome: Gregorian University, 1936, 1946, 1957), p. xix; P. Mandonnet, *Des Ecrits Authentiques de S. Thomas* (Fribourg, Switzerland: Imprimerie de l'oeuvre de saint Paul, 1910); M. Grabmann, *Die Werke des hl. Thomas von Aquin, Beiträge* XXII, 1-2 (Münster, 1949), pp. 325-328; P. Synave, "Le catalogue officiel des oeuvres de s. Thomas d'Aquin," *Archives d'Histoire Doctrinale et Littéraire du Moyen Âge* III (1928) pp. 27, 55, 57, 59, 98; I. T. Eschmann, "A Catalogue of St.

Thomas' Works," in E. Gilson, *The Christian Philosophy of St. Thomas Aquinas* (New York: Random House, 1956), p. 409, #47.

[18] See Keeler, Introduction, *op. cit.*, pp. xii, xx-xxi; P. Mandonnet, *Siger de Brabant et L'Averroisme Latin au XIIIme Siècle* (Louvain: Institut Supérieur de Philosophie, 1911), pp. 103-110; F. Van Steenberghen, *Siger dans l'Histoire de l'Aristotélisme* (Louvain: Institut Supérieur de Philosophie, 1942), pp. 541, 546-548.

[19] I. Thomas, Introduction to K. Foster and S. Humphries (tr.), *Aristotle's De Anima in the Version of William of Moerbeke and the Commentary of St. Thomas Aquinas* (New Haven: Yale University Press, 1951), p. 17; D. Salman, "Compte Rendu: F. Van Steenberghen, *Les Oeuvres et la Doctrine de Siger de Brabant*," *Bulletin Thomiste* 14-15 (1937-1939), p. 655; Grabmann, *op. cit.*, p. 328.

Commentary on the Sentences (ca. 1254-1256), the *Summa contra Gentiles* (ca. 1258-1264), much of the *Summa Theologiae* (ca. 1266-1273), the *Disputed Questions on Spiritual Creatures* (ca. 1268), and the *Disputed Questions on the Soul* (ca. 1269). It was roughly contemporaneous with another anti-Averroistic work, the *De Aeternitate Mundi contra Murmurantes* (ca. 1270 or 1271). It was perhaps followed by the writing of some of the *Commentary on Aristotle's De Anima* (ca. 1269-1273).[20]

In the manuscripts and the older catalogues the treatise appears under varying titles, for example: *Book* or *Treatise—concerning the Unity of the Intellect, concerning the Intellect, concerning the Multiplication of the Intellect, concerning the One Intellect, concerning the Intellect and the Intelligible—against the Averroists; against the Averroists of Paris; against the Error of the Averroists,* or *of Averroes, against Averroes; Book against the Averroists.* But the title most often found is *Treatise concerning the Unity of the Intellect against the Averroists.* Some scribes, thinking that this title needed a clarification, added an explanatory phrase: "concerning the unity of the intellect against the Averroists, or rather against the unity of the intellect which the Averroists held."[21]

The titles, and a reference to *Averroistae* in the text (in section #17), leave no doubt that it is the Averroists whom St. Thomas is opposing. Attempts have been made to determine more exactly what particular Averroist St. Thomas may have had in mind, for example in #122-123, where he seems to cite a definite individual. Mandonnet thinks that St. Thomas was opposing Siger of Brabant, who was the leader of the Averroists at Paris at that time, and two of the older manuscripts assert this. One is entitled: *The Treatise of Brother Thomas against Master Siger concerning the Unity of the Intellect;* and the other states: "Thomas wrote this against Siger of Brabant and many others, predominant in philosophy at Paris in the year of our Lord, 1270."[22] But no work of Siger that is known thus far seems to be

---

[20] Scholars are not always in agreement on the exact dates for each of these writings; the dates given are approximate. On the dates of St. Thomas' works, see Grabmann, *op. cit.;* Eschmann, *op. cit.;* P. Mandonnet and J. Destrez, *Bibliographie Thomiste* (Kain, Belgium: Le Saulchoir, 1921); A. Walz, "Saint Thomas d'Aquin. Ecrits," in *Dictionnaire de Théologie Catholique* XV, pars 1 (1926) 635-641.

[21] Keeler, *loc. cit.,* p. xvii: "*Liber, Tractatus—de Unitate Intellectus, de In-tellectu, de Multiplicatione Intellectus, de Unico Intellectu, de Intellectu et Intelligibili—contra Averroistas (Parisienses), contra Errorem Averroistarum* vel *Averroim; Liber contra Averroistas.*"—The explanatory phrase is in Mss. o, u, f; see Keeler, *loc. cit.,* p. xviii.

[22] *Ibid.,* pp. xviii-xx. See p. xviii: "Tractatus fratris Thomae contra magistrum Sogerum de unitate intellectus;" colophon C: "Haec scripsit Thomas contra Sigerum de Brabantia et alios plurimos Parisius in philosophia reg-

fully and precisely the work St. Thomas attacks in the body of his treatise. Yet this does not mean that St. Thomas did not oppose Master Siger.

C. The Chronological Relation of St. Thomas' Treatise to Some Works of Siger of Brabant

Siger of Brabant (ca. 1240-1284), a younger contemporary of Thomas, was a teacher of philosophy at Paris, in the Faculty of Arts, in 1266. His unorthodox views were included in both of Bishop Tempier's condemnations: December 10, 1270 and March 7, 1277.[23] His *Tractatus de Anima Intellectiva* was thought by Mandonnet to be the work that St. Thomas attacked,[24] but later research has shown that it was composed after St. Thomas' treatise. The *De Unitate Intellectus*, scholars have said, does not seem to reflect the *De Anima Intellectiva;* there is no point by point refutation as one might expect in a work of this kind.[25] Van Steenberghen adds that if it were a reply, it would be absolutely inadequate and insufficient.[26] Rather, the *De Anima Intellectiva* reflects a knowledge of the *De Unitate Intellectus*. In Question III Siger states part of the position of Thomas and comments that Thomas does not philosophize according to the mind of Aristotle; in Question VII he borrows his statement of objections and difficulties from Thomas.[27] Van Steenberghen concludes that the *De Anima Intellectiva* was composed after the *De Unitate Intellectus* of St. Thomas.[28]

But if the *De Anima Intellectiva* followed St. Thomas' treatise, the question, "What work of Siger was St. Thomas opposing?" still remains to be answered.

Perhaps it was a work, no longer extant, that is cited in the *Quodlibeta* of John of Baconthorp, a fourteenth century Carmelite. Chossat points out that the Siger cited in Baconthorp thought, for example, that the intellect is united with man only by means of phantasms, and that, according to Aristotle, only the passive intellect or imaginative power

entes, anno D.ni. 1270." See also Mandonnet, *Siger de Brabant,* pp. 110, 132.

[23] E. Gilson, *History of Christian Philosophy in the Middle Ages* (New York: Random House, 1955), p. 718; A. Maurer, *Mediaeval Philosophy* (New York: Random House, 1962), pp. 407-408.

[24] Mandonnet, *Siger de Brabant,* pp. 110, 132.

[25] P. Doncoeur, "Notes sur les Averroistes Latins," *Revue des Sciences Philosophiques et Théologiques* 4 (1910), p. 501, cited approvingly by M. Chossat, "Saint Thomas d'Aquin

et Siger de Brabant," *Revue de Philosophie* 24 (1914), pp. 563-565. F. Bruckmüller, *Untersuchungen über Sigers (von Brabant) De Anima Intellectiva* (Munich, 1908), had thought the *De Anima Intellectiva* was not even an Averroist work, but Chossat, *art. cit.,* p. 568, thinks this conclusion is not established.

[26] Van Steenberghen, *Siger dans l'Histoire de l'Aristotélisme,* p. 552.

[27] Siger de Brabant, *De Anima Intellectiva,* III & VII in Mandonnet, *op. cit.,* pp. 154, 165-167, 168-169.

[28] Van Steenberghen, *op. cit.,* pp. 553-554.

is the form of man, not the intellective soul or possible intellect. This Siger also implied that the intellect is a mover just as, in Averroes' context, the intelligence that moves the heavens is, without being a form, a principle of operation for the heavens.[29] Chossat concludes that the Siger of Baconthorp closely resembles the Siger that St. Thomas refutes. He adds that without a knowledge of Baconthorp's Siger, one might think the first part of the *De Unitate* captious, entangled, and insistent beyond reason on points which seem evident, but with such a knowledge one sees St. Thomas' treatise as well ordered and adapted to refuting the errors of Siger.[30]

Another work which may also have been an object of St. Thomas' attack is the *Quaestiones in Tertium de Anima*. This work, which is dated before 1270 and is averroistic in content, is also attributed to Siger.[31] Van Steenberghen describes and summarizes these unedited questions but cannot say definitely whether they were known to St. Thomas. He observes, however, that one can find in the *De Unitate* echoes of some of the texts from these questions, notably Siger's discussion on whether the separated soul can suffer from fire.[32]

Van Steenberghen concludes, then, that two psychological writings of Siger existed prior to the *De Unitate*. This does not mean that they were necessarily true publications of Siger. They might have existed only in the form of *reportationes* of students. Van Steenberghen sees evidence of this in the *Quaestiones in Tertium de Anima*.[33] If it be true that St. Thomas' sources were students' notes of Siger's oral teaching, this would explain, says Van Steenberghen, the double fact that St. Thomas seems to use and refute a text and yet reproaches his opponent for not rendering his teaching public and controllable.[34] Although

---

[29] Chossat, *art. cit.*, pp. 558-563. John of Baconthorp, *Quodlibeta* I, 1 (Venice, 1527), fol. 2vb, 3ra-rb. See St. Thomas, *De Unitate Intellectus*, #3-79, esp. #17, 63, 67.

[30] Chossat, *art. cit.*, pp. 563-565.

[31] J. J. Duin, *La Doctrine de la Providence dans les Écrits de Siger de Brabant* (Louvain: Institut Supérieur de Philosophie, 1954), dates this work before 1271 and includes Question 2 in his book, pp. 57-60, 402. Van Steenberghen, *Siger dans l'Histoire de L'Aristotélisme*, dates the work 1265-1270 (p. 564), discusses its authenticity (p. 514), and summarizes it (pp. 630-632); in *Siger de Brabant: Les Oeuvres Inédites* (1931), he gives citations from it and a description of the content of each question, pp. 164-177.

[32] Van Steenberghen, *Siger dans l'Histoire de l'Aristotélisme*, p. 558. See *Quaestiones in Tertium de Anima*, q. 11, in *Siger de Brabant: Les Oeuvres Inédites*, pp. 170-171, and St. Thomas, *De Unitate Intellectus*, #123.

[33] Van Steenberghen, *Siger dans l'Histoire . . .*, pp. 528, 557.

[34] *Ibid.*, p. 557. The latter part of Van Steenberghen's comment is a reference to *De Un. Int.* #124: ". . . let him not speak in corners, nor in the presence of boys who do not know how to judge about such difficult matters; but let him write against this treatise if he dares. . . ." This may not merely be a criticism of the adversary expressing his views only in oral teaching to young people, rather than expressing them also in

the *De Unitate* was probably directed against many Averroists at Paris, it may well have attacked in particular the doctrines of Siger as known through notes of his oral teachings.

In the final paragraph of the *De Unitate* St. Thomas issues a challenge. Speaking of his opponent he says: ". . . let him write against this treatise if he dares."(#124) Was the challenge ever accepted? Did Siger ever answer St. Thomas' *De Unitate?*

We have noted that the *De Anima Intellectiva* was written after the *De Unitate* and reveals a knowledge of some of the content of St. Thomas' treatise. Was the *De Anima Intellectiva* then intended as Siger's answer to the *De Unitate?*

Sylvester of Ferrare, O.P. (ca. 1474-1528) tells of a Siger who ". . . sent to blessed Thomas his treatise *De Intellectu,* in answer to the *Treatise against the Averroists.*"[35] Chossat identified this *De Intellectu* with the *De Anima Intellectiva.*[36] Other scholars (notably Bruno Nardi) have more recently thought that Siger wrote, after 1271, a *De Intellectu* that was distinct from the *De Anima Intellectiva.* Augustino Nifo (1473-ca. 1538) affirmed that Siger had sent a treatise, *De Intellectu,* to Thomas in answer to the treatise against the Averroists. Nifo's comments on the contents of the *De Intellectu* strongly suggest that it is different from the *De Anima Intellectiva* and that it manifests a particular interest in the possible intellect.[37] Perhaps then it was

formally written treatises to which everyone has access. It may imply, too, that the oral teaching of the Averroists was imparted to small groups in private places. Keeler notes, *op. cit.,* p. 80, that as late as September 2, 1276, this decree was issued (Denifle & Chatelain, *Chartularium Universitatis Parisiensis* I, 539): "Thus it is that we, in reference to secret small gatherings for teaching, which are forbidden by the sacred canons and are inimical to wisdom, decree and ordain that no master or bachelor, of any faculty whatever, may receive groups to read in private places away from everyone else, because of the many dangers which can result from this, but they must hold their meetings in common places where all can come who will be able to report faithfully on the things which are being taught there; we make exception, however, for grammatical and logical readings, in which there can be no excessive boldness."

[35] Franciscus Sylvester Ferrariensis, *Commentaria in Summam contra Gentiles* III, 45; IV, 2 (in Leonine edition of St. Thomas, XIV, p. 119, col. 2). Sylvester speaks of *Rugerius,* but this is regarded as an evident corruption of *Sigerius.* See Van Steenberghen, *Siger dans l'Histoire* . . ., p. 553 and note 3.

[36] Chossat, *art. cit.,* p. 570.

[37] B. Nardi, *Sigieri di Brabante nel Pensiero del Rinascimento Italiano* (Rome, 1945), pp. 19-26; E. Gilson, *History of Christian Philosophy in the Middle Ages,* pp. 396-397, gives a translation of Nardi's summary of the main positions of the "lost" *De Intellectu;* see also Gilson, *op. cit.,* pp. 722-723, notes 28-30; on the distinctness of the *De Intellectu* and the *De Anima Intellectiva,* see G. da Palma, *La Dottrina sull' Unita' dell' Intelletto in Sigieri di Brabante* (Padua: Casa Editrice Dott. Antonio Milani, 1955), pp. 29-30.

this *De Intellectu,* known now only in the fragments preserved by Nifo, that was written by Siger in answer, or partly in answer, to the *De Unitate,* and perhaps in the years 1272-1273, after St. Thomas had left Paris for Italy.[38]

The *De Anima Intellectiva,* which refers to Thomas in Questions III and VII, may perhaps have been written between 1273-1276.[39] In this work Siger speaks of the intellective soul as a form, not a mover. This contrast with the views of the Siger of Baconthorp and the Siger of the *Quaestiones in Tertium de Anima,* does not mean that he now accepted a Thomistic position, since this form that he speaks of in the *De Anima Intellectiva* is a *forma intrinsecus operans,* a form intrinsically united to the body for operation. It operates within man in order to know, although it is separate in its being from the body.[40]

A work entitled *Quaestiones in Libros Tres Aristotelis de Anima* has also been attributed to Siger.[41] Published by Van Steenberghen, these questions, which should not be confused with the *Quaestiones in Tertium de Anima,* express a doctrine of the intellective soul that is very close to that of St. Thomas. Relying on these texts, Van Steenberghen

---

[38] Nardi, *op. cit.,* p. 33, thinks that the *De Intellectu* must have been written before the *De Anima Intellectiva.* On the date of the *De Intellectu,* see da Palma, *op. cit.,* p. 29.

[39] See da Palma, *op. cit.,* pp. 29-30. Van Steenberghen, *Siger dans l'Histoire* . . ., pp. 553-554, had dated the *De Anima Intellectiva* 1272 or 1273, but this was on Chossat's supposition that the *De Anima Intellectiva* is identical with the *De Intellectu* mentioned by Sylvester of Ferrare; Van Steenberghen does, however, note the difficulties encountered in accepting this supposition.

—It should be noted that Jean of Jandun (d. 1328) also refers to a treatise on the intellect by Siger. Although the name is given as "Remigius," it is clearly Siger who is intended; Nardi, *op. cit.,* p. 21, notes that some manuscripts state more accurately: "Segerus" or "Sirges." The relevant text is as follows: "Et debes scire quod istam solutionem hujus rationis, qualiter homo intelligit ad aliquid, posuit Reverendus doctor Philosophiae magister Remigius de Brabantia in quodam suo Tractatu de intellectu, qui sic incipit: *Cum anima sit aliorum cognoscitiva. . . .*" (Jean of Jandun, *Quaestiones de*

Anima III, 5 (Venice, 1552) fol. 60ra.) Because the *incipit* is the same as that of the *De Anima Intellectiva,* this *De Intellectu* is regarded as identical with the *De Anima Intellectiva.* See S. MacClintock, *Perversity and Error: Studies on the "Averroist" John of Jandun* (Bloomington, Ind.: Indiana University Press, 1956), pp. 57, 156, note 21; Chossat, *art. cit.,* pp. 569-575; Van Steenberghen, *Siger dans l'Histoire* . . ., pp. 552-553.

[40] Siger, *De Anima Intellectiva* III, in Mandonnet, *op. cit.,* pp. 154-155; Gilson, *op. cit.,* pp. 397-398, 723-724, note 31; A. Maurer, *op. cit.,* p. 198. Van Steenberghen, *Siger dans l'Histoire* . . ., p. 647, suggests that Siger may have seen in the doctrine of the *forma intrinsecus operans* a compromise between the position of Averroes and that of Thomas Aquinas, but it was only a verbal solution, since in the context of an Aristotelian metaphysics there can be no middle position between a substantial union and a purely operative union that can be only an accidental union.

[41] *Quaestiones in Libros Tres Aristotelis de Anima,* in Van Steenberghen, *Siger de Brabant: Les Oeuvres Inédites,* pp. 11-160.

suggests that the last stage in the evolution of Siger's thought on the soul and the intellect, was a conversion to Thomism.[42] But because the attribution of these questions to Siger has been criticized for serious reasons, this work cannot be listed among the certainly authentic writings of Siger.[43]

Because much research still needs to be done on problems of the authenticity and chronology of works attributed to Siger, the relation of Siger's writings to St. Thomas' treatise cannot be stated in a definitive way. Tentatively, however, the sequence of works perhaps could be summarized thus:

1) The Siger mentioned by Baconthorp
2) Siger's *Quaestiones in Tertium de Anima*
   (in the form of *reportationes*)
3) St. Thomas' *De Unitate Intellectus contra Averroistas*
4) Siger's *De Intellectu*, (as known through Nifo's references to it)
5) Siger's *De Anima Intellectiva*
6) *Quaestiones in Libros Tres Aristotelis de Anima*
   (attributed to Siger by Van Steenberghen, but its authenticity is disputed.)

According to Sylvester of Ferrare, Siger's *De Intellectu* was sent to Thomas, who had left for Italy in 1272. We do not know whether St. Thomas ever received that work or whether he saw any part of the *De Anima Intellectiva*. Chossat conjectures that perhaps it may have seemed futile to Thomas to continue the dialogue since the reworded version of Siger's position offered nothing basically new, or perhaps death may have come (March 7, 1274) before St. Thomas had time to answer.[44]

D. THE CONTENT AND STRUCTURE OF ST. THOMAS' TREATISE

St. Thomas begins the *De Unitate Intellectus contra Averroistas* with a statement of his purpose and his method of procedure in this work. Although he has written before against Averroes' erroneous view on the intellect, he intends to write against it again and clearly refute it. He is concerned about the spread of this error and the boldness of those who expound it. He distinguishes two aspects of the error: (1) that the possible intellect is a substance that is separate in its being from the body and not united to it as its form; and (2) that this possible intellect is one for all men.

---

[42] Van Steenberghen, *Siger de Brabant dans l'Histoire* . . ., pp. 510, 515-527. 653-662. Van Steenberghen, p. 564, dates this work 1275-1277.
[43] Gilson, "Compte Rendu," *Bulletin Thomiste* 6 (1940-1942) 5-22; Gilson, "Concerning the Thomism of

Siger of Brabant, "in *Dante, the Philosopher* (New York: Sheed & Ward, 1949), pp. 317-327; A. Maurer, "The State of Historical Research in Siger of Brabant," *Speculum* 31 (January, 1956) 49-56.
[44] Chossat, *art. cit.*, p. 575.

His method of procedure will not be to show that the error is contrary to the teachings of the Christian Faith, for this is quite evident. He intends instead to show that the error is against the principles of philosophy and against the words of those very Peripatetics to whom these men appeal. He will therefore challenge them on their own ground by using philosophical arguments and the method of textual analysis.

The two aspects of Averroes' error provide the two main parts of the body of the treatise, with the first three chapters pertaining to the first aspect of the error, and the last two chapters pertaining to its second aspect. The division into five chapters is found in the older editions and in manuscripts and, in Keeler's opinion, was probably made by St. Thomas himself.[45] The relation of the five chapters to the two main parts of the body of the treatise is presented in this way by Keeler:[46]

I. The possible intellect is not a substance that is separate in its being.
This is proved
(Chapter I) by the authority of Aristotle,
(Chapter II) and of other Peripatetics;
(Chapter III) by arguments from reason.
II. The possible intellect is not one in all men.
This is established
(Chapter IV) by arguments, especially from Aristotle,
(Chapter V) by refutations of the adversaries' arguments.

In dealing with the first aspect of Averroes' error, namely, that the intellect is a substance separate in its being from the body, St. Thomas begins with an analysis of Aristotle's texts (Chapter I, sections #3-30) in order to show that this is not the Philosopher's view. So thorough and detailed is the analysis that St. Thomas gives the impression of not omitting any text to which his opponents appealed in support of their views. For them the Philosopher's way of defining the soul implied that the intellective faculty or intellect was excluded from his definitions. For St. Thomas, Aristotle's definitions of soul included the intellect, and the reference to intellect as "separate" meant not separate from the body, but different from sense powers in that it has no corporeal organ. (#25-26)

Among the objections that St. Thomas answers (#31-50), is one that especially reflects the Averroists' view. Assuming that there are

[45] Keeler, Introduction, *op. cit.*, p. xviii.
[46] *Ibid.* Keeler refers the reader to the analytical tables worked out by C. Ottaviano, *Saggio Contra la Dott.* *Averr. Dell' Unità dell' Int.* (Lanciano, 1930), pp. 83-85. See also the analysis of Van Steenberghen, *Siger dans l'Histoire* . . ., pp. 633-636.

only two kinds of forms, spiritual forms totally separate from matter, and material forms immersed in matter, the Averroists wondered: How can the intellect be a power of a soul that is the form of the body? On this supposition, would it not be immersed in matter and so be unable to know? Or, differently phrased: How can the human soul be so intimately united with the body as to be its substantial form and yet have one of its powers so separate from the body that that power can have intellectual knowledge? The answer lay, St. Thomas thought, in acknowledging another kind of form of matter. Although some forms of matter neither act by themselves nor exist by themselves, but exist only through the composite, there are other forms of matter that do act by themselves and hence are subsistent. They do not exist through the composite, but the composite exists through them. Not being immersed in matter, they can have acts that are not acts of a corporeal organ. (#28, 30, 37-38, 42) The human soul is this unique kind of form of matter.

At the end of the first chapter St. Thomas says (#50): ". . . from this careful consideration of almost all the words of Aristotle concerning the human intellect it is clear that he was of the opinion that the human soul is the act of the body, and that the possible intellect is a part or power of that soul."

In Chapter II (#51-59) St. Thomas wishes to show that the Greek and Arabian Peripatetics to whom his opponents appeal, also regarded the possible intellect as a part of the human soul and not as a separate substance. In presenting the views of two of the Greeks, St. Thomas has a special advantage over his adversaries. Instead of relying on Averroes' mention of them, St. Thomas makes use of William of Moerbeke's recent translation of Themistius' *De Anima*. He cites some texts in which Themistius states his own view and that of Theophrastus, and thereby tries to establish that for both, the intellect is a power of the human soul. (#51-55) For Alexander of Aphrodisias he notes that even Averroes admitted that Alexander regarded the possible intellect as the form of the body. (#56)

While admitting that Avicenna's position is not completely in harmony with the view of soul as substantial form, he notes that Avicenna did hold that the intellect is a power of man's soul, and that Algazel acknowledged an operative and a cognitive power as powers of the soul. (#57-58)

St. Thomas states that he has referred to the Greeks and the Arabs not because he wishes to rely upon their authority; rather he wishes to show his opponents that not only the Latin philosophers but also the Greeks and the Arabs whom they hold in esteem, regarded the intellect as a power of the soul. He wonders from which Peripatetics they have taken their error, and then adds, in sharp terms, "unless perchance they are less willing to be right with other Peripatetics than to be wrong with Averroes, who was not so much a Peripatetic as a perverter of Peripatetic philosophy." (#59)

In Chapter III (#60-85) St. Thomas gives philosophical arguments to show that the intellect is a power of the soul which is the form of the body. His principal argument starts from the evident fact that this individual man knows *(Hic homo singularis intelligit)*. (#62) After stating Averroes' account of how this man knows (#63), he rejects it, stressing especially that in Averroes' context, man is not really a knower but the intellect's object of knowledge. (#63-66)

Seeing that Averroes has not explained how this man knows, some have suggested a variation of the Commentator's account. They said that the intellect is united to the individual as a mover and therefore the man knows. But what is the individual man in this context? St. Thomas asks. Is he intellect alone *(motor)*, or a body animated by a vegetative and sensitive soul *(motum)*, or the composite resulting from the union of mover and moved? (#67) After a careful critique of these three hypotheses (#68-78), St. Thomas concludes that one cannot say that the intellect is united to man as a mover, and even if it were, this would not explain that this individual man knows. (#79)

Besides this psychological argument, St. Thomas presents, though more briefly, two other arguments to show that the intellect cannot be a substance that is separate in its being from the body. Since the distinguishing act of man's species is the act of understanding, the principle of this act, that is the intellective soul, must be united to man's body as its form. (#80) The other argument based on requirements of the moral order points out that if the intellect were separate, then the will would also be separate. But then man would not be the master of his acts, and the basis of moral philosophy would be destroyed. (#81-82)

St. Thomas concludes this chapter by refuting objections of the Averroists. (#83-85) In giving his answers he stresses again the importance of grasping that the soul, though a form of matter, is not a material form. (#83-84)

Having completed his discussion of the first aspect of Averroes' error, that the intellect is a substance separate in its being from the body, St. Thomas proceeds in Chapter IV (#86-98) to consider the second aspect of the error: that the intellect is one for all men. He remarks that although something can perhaps be said for the unity of the agent intellect, to say that the possible intellect is one for all men involves absurd consequences. Among the consequences that he discusses (#86-91) is that there would then be but one knowing being

[14]

and one act of understanding and willing. This view then fails to account for the obvious diversity of acts of knowing and willing. Besides, it is contrary to the teachings of Aristotle (#92-96); even if it were not, no matter how the relation of the one intellect to our phantasms is explained in Averroes' context, Averroes' doctrine cannot account for the fact that man knows. (#96-98)

In Chapter V (#99-124) St. Thomas tries to understand why the Averroists are opposed to a doctrine of the plurality of possible intellects. He states and answers several objections. The Averroists argue, for example, that because the thing understood is one, therefore the intellect must be one. St. Thomas shows that they prove too much, for they should conclude then not only that there is one intellect for all men, but that there is only one intellect in the whole universe, thus denying plurality to separate substances. (#107) St. Thomas tries to probe to the source of their difficulty by asking what they mean by "the thing understood." Do they mean a thing outside the mind or species within the mind? The latter is really their meaning, St. Thomas shows, and their trouble arises from not seeing a distinction between the two meanings. (#109-110) St. Thomas tries to show his opponents how one existent thing can be known by many persons by means of the species which each one's intellect has. (#112-113) After the discussion of doctrinal difficulties, St. Thomas again calls attention to philosophers' actual texts. He stresses that the Greeks and the Arabs to whom his opponents mistakenly appeal in support of their error, have all upheld a plurality of possible intellects. (#119-121)

In the last two sections (#122-123) of this part, St. Thomas addresses a more direct and theological criticism to his opponents and to one unnamed Averroist in particular. What disturbs St. Thomas even more than their error concerning one intellect, is the irreverent attitude they have towards the Christian Faith. To say, as one Averroist does: "I necessarily conclude through reason that the intellect is one in number; but I firmly hold the opposite through faith," is to imply that faith is concerned with something false and impossible. To so oppose reason and faith, and to dispute about matters of faith that do not pertain to philosophy, is unbecoming to Christians.

In the last section of the *De Unitate* (#124) St. Thomas restates (from #2) the method he has used to refute the Averroists' error; he has appealed, in the body of his treatise, not to the teachings of faith but to the arguments and words of the philosophers themselves. St. Thomas concludes his treatise by issuing a challenge in unusually strong and vigorous language: ". . . if there be anyone boasting of his knowledge, falsely so-called, who wishes to say something against what we have written here, let him not speak in corners, nor in the presence

[15]

of boys who do not know how to judge about such difficult matters; but let him write against this treatise if he dares; and he will find not only me who am the least of others, but many other lovers of truth, by whom his error will be opposed, or his ignorance remedied."

The following outline may serve as a summary of the principal divisions and subdivisions of St. Thomas' treatise:

An Outline of the *De Unitate Intellectus contra Averroistas*

[16]

2. Unicity of the intellect is incompatible with Aristotle's doctrine: #92-96
3. No matter how the relation of the intellect to our phantasms is understood, the doctrine of one possible intellect for all men cannot explain human knowledge: #96-98

B. Objections against the plurality of possible intellects, and refutations of these objections: Chapter V: #99-121

C. Special criticism of Christian Averroists: Chapter V: #122-123

IV. Conclusion of the Treatise: #124

Although the *De Unitate Intellectus* was written to answer a definite problem of St. Thomas' time, it was not just an occasional or ephemeral work. It touches upon some very basic and vital questions which surpass in their reach, the limits of a thirteenth century polemic. For example:

(1) What is the soul?
(2) What powers does the human soul have?
(3) What is the relation of the intellect to the human soul?
(4) How is the intellective power like the senses, and how is it unlike the senses?
(5) What is meant by saying that the soul is the form of the body?
(6) Why can it not be said that the soul is related to the body as a mover?
(7) How can the soul be the form of the body and yet some power of the soul not be a power of the body?
(8) How can the soul be so intimately united with the body as to be its form and yet be so separate from the body as to be able to exist without it?
(9) Is every form of matter a material form?
(10) What is meant by saying that matter is a principle of individuation?
(11) What are the moral implications of the view that there is one possible intellect for all men?
(12) Can anything be said in favor of the view that there is one agent intellect for all men?
(13) What is the nature of knowing?
(14) Is knowledge a transitive or an immanent action?
(15) What is "the thing understood": a thing in itself, or a thing-in-the-mind?
(16) What is meant by abstraction?
(17) What is meant by intelligible species?
(18) What is meant by teaching? by learning?
(19) How can many persons know one thing?
(20) How does knowledge exist in us when we are not actually knowing?
(21) Can God do what is contradictory or impossible?
(22) Can reason demonstrate the truth of a proposition that is contrary to faith?

(23) Is reason competent to deal with every question?
(24) What is the relation between faith and reason?

St. Thomas' treatment of these and other questions in the *De Unitate* is notable for its clarity of expression and the depth of his philosophical insight.

E. The Present Translation

There have been many editions of the *De Unitate Intellectus*. Father Leo W. Keeler, S.J., gives a history of these editions from the *incunabula* through the editions of the first three decades of the twentieth century.[47] He studied over twenty manuscripts and early editions to establish the text for his own edition, which was first published at Rome and reprinted in 1946 and 1957.[48] It has been described as a "very good" and "thoroughly reliable" edition.[49]

This volume contains an English translation of Father Keeler's edition of St. Thomas' text. It includes Keeler's section numbers to facilitate reference to the text, and Keeler's titles for chapters and parts of chapters. Although using Keeler's notes as a guide, it does not reproduce them exactly. It utilizes, for example, more recent editions of Averroes' *Commentary on Aristotle's De Anima* and of William of Moerbeke's translation of Themistius' *Commentary*.

The bibliography which follows in Section F, is intended to direct the reader to works that will aid in the understanding of the background and content of the *De Unitate,* and of some of the main problems with which the treatise is concerned.

F. Selected Bibliography

Aristotle, *De Anima*, tr. J. A. Smith, in *The Basic Works of Aristotle*, ed. R. McKeon. New York: Random House, 1941.
Averroes, *Commentarium Magnum in Aristotelis de Anima Libros,* ed. F. S. Crawford. Cambridge, Mass.: Mediaeval Academy of America, 1953.
Chossat, M., "Saint Thomas d'Aquin et Siger de Brabant," *Revue de Philosophie* 24 (1914), 533-575; 25 (1914) 25-52.
Gilson, E., *History of Christian Philosophy in the Middle Ages,* Part Nine, Chapters I-II. New York: Random House, 1955.
————. *The Christian Philosophy of St. Thomas Aquinas,* Part Two, Chapters IV-VI. New York: Random House, 1956.
————. *Elements of Christian Philosophy,* Chapters 9-10. New York: Doubleday & Co., 1960.
————. *The Spirit of Mediaeval Philosophy,* Chapter IX. New York: Scribner's, 1936.
Keeler, L. W., S.J., "History of the Editions of St. Thomas' 'De unitate intellectus,' " *Gregorianum* 17 (1936), 53-81.
————. *Sancti Thomae Aquinatis Tractatus de Unitate Intellectus contra Averroistas,* Introduction and notes. Rome: Gregorian University, 1936, 1946, 1957.

[47] Keeler, "History of the Editions of the *De Unitate Intellectus,*" *Gregorianum* 17 (Jan.-Mar., 1936) 53-81.
[48] Keeler, *Sancti Thomae Aquinatis Tractatus de Unitate Intellectus contra Averroistas:* Editio Critica. (Rome: Gregorian University, 1936, 1946, 1957).
[49] Van Steenberghen, *Siger dans l'Histoire . . .,* p. 633, note 2; Eschmann, *op. cit.,* p. 409.

Mandonnet, P., *Siger de Brabant et l'Averroisme Latin au XIIIme Siècle*. Louvain: Institut Supérieur de Philosophie, 1911.

Pegis, A.C., "St. Thomas and the Unity of Man," pp. 153-173, in *Progress in Philosophy*, ed. J. A. McWilliams. Milwaukee: Bruce, 1955.

———. "Some Reflections on *Summa contra Gentiles* II, 56," pp. 169-188, in *An Etienne Gilson Tribute*, ed. C. J. O'Neil. Milwaukee: Marquette University Press, 1959.

Robb, J. H., "Intelligere Intelligentibus Est Esse," pp. 209-227, in *An Etienne Gilson Tribute*, ed. C. J. O'Neil. Milwaukee: Marquette University Press, 1959.

Thomas Aquinas, St. *Tractatus de Unitate Intellectus contra Averroistas*, critical edition by L. W. Keeler, S.J. Rome: Gregorian University, 1936, 1946, 1957.

———. *The Soul: A Translation of St. Thomas Aquinas' De Anima*, by J. P. Rowan. St. Louis: Herder, 1949.

———. *Aristotle's De Anima with the Commentary of St. Thomas Aquinas*, tr. K. Foster and S. Humphries. New Haven: Yale University Press, 1951.

———. *On Spiritual Creatures*, tr. M. C. Fitzpatrick and J. J. Wellmuth. Milwaukee: Marquette University Press, 1949.

———. *Summa contra Gentiles*, II, 49-89, in *On the Truth of the Catholic Faith*, II, tr. J. F. Anderson. New York: Doubleday Image Books, 1956.

———. *Summa Theologiae* I, pp. 75-89, in *Basic Writings of St. Thomas Aquinas*, I, tr. A. C. Pegis. New York: Random House, 1945.

Van Steenberghen, F., *Siger dans l'Histoire de l'Aristotélisme*, vol. II of *Siger de Brabant* (Les Philosophes Belges, Tome XIII), esp. pp. 633-641. Louvain: Institut Supérieur de Philosophie, 1942.

———. *Aristotle in the West*, tr. L. Johnston. Louvain: Nauwelaerts, 1955.

Verbeke, G., "Thémistius et le 'De Unitate Intellectus' de saint Thomas," pp. xxxix-lxii, in *Thémistius: Commentaire sur le Traité de l'Âme d'Aristote: Traduction de Guillaume de Moerbeke*. Louvain: Publications Universitaires de Louvain, 1957.

———. "L'Unité de l'Homme: saint Thomas contre Averroès," *Revue Philosophique de Louvain* 58 (III série, no. 58, 1960) 220-249.

ON THE UNITY OF THE INTELLECT AGAINST THE AVERROISTS

(De Unitate Intellectus Contra Averroistas)

by

Saint Thomas Aquinas

#1-2. Foreword[1]

#1. Just as all men naturally desire to know the truth,[2] so there is inherent in men a natural desire to avoid errors, and refute them when they are able to do so. Now among other errors, the error that seems especially inappropriate is the one concerning that very intellect through which we are meant by nature to avoid errors and know the truth.

For a long time now there has been spreading among many people an error concerning the intellect, arising from the words of Averroes.[3] He tries to assert that the intellect that Aristotle calls the possible intellect,[4] but that he himself calls by the unsuitable name "material," is a substance separate in its being from the body and not united to it in some way as its form,[5] and furthermore that this possible intellect is one for all men.[6] Against these views we have already written many

---

[1] Throughout this translation the headings given in parentheses are Keeler's headings. The numbers preceded by "#" are Keeler's section numbers.

[2] Aristotle, *Metaphysics* I, 1, 980a.

[3] On the rise of Latin Averroism, see Introduction, Part A.

[4] Aristotle, *De Anima* III, 4, 429a 18-24.

[5] The term, "material intellect," was used by Alexander of Aphrodisias, *De Intellectu et Intellecto*, in G. Théry, *Alexandre d'Aphrodise* (Kain, Belgium: Le Saulchoir, 1926), p. 74. In his *Commentarium Magnum in Aristotelis de Anima Libros* Averroes cites Alexander's views, borrows his term, but differs from him on the nature of the material or possible intellect; see (in the critical edition of The Mediaeval Academy of America, Cambridge, Mass., 1953) *In de Anima* II, comm. 32, p. 178; III, comm. 5, pp. 388, 393-398; comm. 14, pp. 431-432; comm. 20, pp. 446-448, 453; comm. 25, p. 463; comm. 36, p. 498. The Mediaeval Academy edition of Averroes' *Commentary on the De Anima* will be cited throughout these notes.

[6] Averroes, *In de Anima* III, comm. 5, pp. 411-413.

things in the past.[7] But because the boldness of those who err has not ceased to strive against the truth, we will try again to write something against this same error to refute it clearly.

#2. It is not now our intention to show that the above-mentioned position is erroneous in this, that it is opposed to the truth of the Christian Faith. For this can easily enough become evident to everyone. For if we deny to men a diversity of the intellect, which alone among the parts of the soul seems to be incorruptible and immortal, it follows that after death nothing of the souls of men would remain except that single substance of intellect; and so the recompense of rewards and punishments and also their diversity would be destroyed.

However, we intend to show that the above-mentioned position is no less against the principles of philosophy than against the teachings of Faith. And because, so they say, the words of the Latins on this subject have no savor for some persons, but these men say that they follow the words of the Peripatetics, whose books on this subject they have never seen, except those of Aristotle who was the founder of the Peripatetic Sect;[8] we shall show first that the above-mentioned position is entirely opposed to his words and meaning.

---

[7] See *Scriptum super Libros Sententiarum, In II Sent.*, d. 17, q. 2, a. 1; *Summa contra Gentiles* II, 59-61, 68-70, 73, 75, 77-78; *Summa Theologiae* I, q. 76, a. 1 & 2; *Quaestiones Disputatae de Anima*, a. 2 & 3; *De Spiritualibus Creaturis*, a. 2 & 9; *In Aristotelis Librum de Anima Commentarium* III, lectio 7 & 8. This commentary may have been written after the *De Unitate Intellectus;* see Introduction, Part B.

[8] Keeler remarks that with exaggerated irony St. Thomas accuses the Averroists of knowing authorities only as they were quoted by Averroes, who himself "was not so much a Peripatetic as a perverter of Peripatetic philosophy." (#59)

CHAPTER I.

(#3-50. Aristotle did not teach that the possible intellect is a substance separate in its being from the body.)

(#3-4. The definition of the soul that Aristole gives, belongs also to the intellective soul.)

#3. The first definition of the soul that Aristotle sets down in Book II of the *De Anima,* saying that "the soul is the first act of a physical organic body,"[1] should be accepted. And lest perhaps someone might say that this definition does not apply to every soul[2] because of the fact that Aristotle had previously qualified his treatment by saying: "If it is necessary to say that there is something common to every soul,"[3] which they interpret as meaning that this could not be, the words of his that follow should be accepted. For he says: "It has been stated in a universal way what the soul is. For a substance is what it is by definition; now this is the essence of this body,"[4] that is, the substantial form of a physical organic body.

#4. And lest perhaps it be said that the intellective part is excluded from this universal statement, this is answered by what he says afterwards: "It is indeed clear therefore that the soul is not separable from the body, or that certain of the soul's parts are [not separable], if it naturally has parts, for it is the act of the certain parts themselves. But truly nothing prevents certain parts [from being separable] since they are not the acts of any body."[5] This cannot be understood except with reference to the intellect and will, which pertain to the intellective part. From this it is clearly shown concerning that soul which Aristotle had defined above in a universal way as the act of the body, that it has some parts which are acts of some parts of the body, but also some which are acts of no body. For it is one thing for the soul to be the act of the body and another for part of it to be the act of the body, as will be shown later.[6] Whence also in this same chapter he shows that the soul is the act of the body in this that some of its parts are acts of the body, when he says: "It is necessary to consider with regard to the parts what has been said,"[7] namely in the whole.

---

[1] Aristotle, *De Anima* II, 1, 412b 5. (See St. Thomas, *Comm. in de Anima* II, lect. 1, 212; lect. 4, 271.)

[2] See Averroes, *In de Anima* II, comm. 7, p. 138, lines 15-19; III, comm. 5, p. 397, lines 296-298.

[3] Aristotle, *De Anima* II, 1, 412b 4.

[4] *Ibid.,* 412b 10-12.

[5] *Ibid.,* 413a 3-7.

[6] In *De Unitate Intellectus,* #27-28.

[7] Aristotle, *De Anima* II, 1, 412b 23-24.

(#5-11. For the soul is also said to be that by which we first live and understand.)

#5. But it becomes still clearer from what follows that the intellect is also included under this general definition. For although he has sufficiently proved that the soul is the act of the body (since when the soul is separate from it, the body is not actually living),[8] yet something can be said to be actually such by the presence of something, not only if it is a form but also if it is a mover (just as what is combustible is actually burned by the presence of something burning, and whatever is movable is actually moved by the presence of something moving). For this reason someone could come to doubt whether a body is actually living by the presence of a soul in the way in which what is movable is actually moved by the presence of a mover, or in the way in which matter is in act by the presence of form. And especially because Plato held that the soul is not united to the body as its form but rather as its mover and ruler, as is clear through Plotinus and Gregory of Nyssa;[9] (I mention these because they were not Latins but Greeks). This doubt therefore is what the Philosopher is hinting at when he adds to what he has said: "But further, it is unclear whether the soul is the act of the body in the way that a sailor is of a ship."[10]

#6. Then because after what he had said, this doubt still remained, he concludes: "The soul is thus indeed defined and described in a general way,"[11] because he had not yet clearly demonstrated the truth.

To remove this doubt therefore, he next proceeds to show that which is more certain both in itself and in knowledge, through those things that are less certain in themselves but more certain to us, that is, through the effects of the soul which are the acts of the soul. Then he at once distinguishes the works of the soul, saying that "the animate is distinguished from the inanimate inasmuch as it is living," and that there are many things which pertain to life, namely, "intellect, sense, motion and position according to place, and the motion of nourishment and growth" so that "in whatever being any of these is found, that thing is said to live."[12] And having shown how these are mutually related, that is how one of these can be without another, he concludes to this effect, "that the soul is the principle of all the foregoing," and that the soul is determined (as by its parts) by the vegetative, sensitive, intellective, and motive,"[13] and that "all these happen to be found in one and the same [principle]," as in man.[14]

---

[8] *Ibid.*, 412b 18 - 413a 4.
[9] Here St. Thomas seems to be referring to passages that he cites in #76, 78. See notes to these sections.
[10] Aristotle, *De Anima* II, 1, 413a 8-9.

[11] *Ibid.*, 413a 9-10.
[12] *Ibid.*, II, 2, 413a 21-25.
[13] *Ibid.*, 413b 11-13.
[14] *Ibid.*, 413b 32.

#7. And Plato held that there are diverse souls in man, according to which distinct vital operations belong to him.[15] Consequently Aristotle raises the question: "whether each of these is soul through itself, or is a part of the soul; and if they are parts of one soul, whether they differ only by reason, or also differ in location," that is, in an organ. And he adds that "in some cases this does not seem difficult, but some cases raise a question."[16] For he shows next what is clear in things which pertain to the vegetative soul, and in things which pertain to the sensitive soul, through this fact that some plants and animals live after they have been cut apart, and all the operations of the soul which belong to the whole, appear in each part.

But he shows which points he considers questionable when he adds that "nothing is as yet evident concerning the intellect and perceiving power."[17] This he does not say with the purpose of showing that the intellect is not the soul, as the Commentator[18] and his followers wrongly teach; for clearly here he is answering what he had said above; for some cases "raise a question." Therefore this should be understood in this way; that it is not yet evident whether the intellect is the soul or part of the soul; and if part of the soul, whether separate in location or only distinct by reason.

#8. And although he says this is not yet clear, yet he shows what is apparent on this point at first glance when he adds: "But it seems to be another genus of soul."[19] This should not be understood as the Commentator and his followers wrongly teach,[20] that this was said for this reason that intellect is used equivocally of soul, or that the above-mentioned definition cannot be applied to it, but how this should be understood appears from what he adds: "And it belongs to this alone to be separated as the eternal from the corruptible."[21] In this respect, therefore, it is another genus because the intellect seems to be something eternal, whereas other parts of the soul are corruptible. And because the corruptible and eternal do not seem able to come together into one substance, it seems that of the parts of the soul, it belongs to this part alone (namely the intellect) to be separated not indeed from the body, as the Commentator wrongly explains,[22] but from the other

---

[15] Plato, *Timaeus* 89E-90A, 69C-70A, in B. Jowett (tr.), *Dialogues of Plato*, III (Oxford: Clarendon Press, 1953); *Phaedrus* 246, 253; *Republic* IV, 435B-442A (in Jowett ed., II). See Aristotle on Plato, in *De Anima* I, 3, 407a 4-6. Averroes cites Plato in *In de Anima* I, comm. 90, p. 121.

[16] Aristotle, *De Anima* II, 2, 413b 13-17. (See St. Thomas, *Comm. in de Anima* II, lect. 4)

[17] Aristotle, *De Anima* II, 2, 413b 17-24.

[18] Averroes, *In de Anima* II, comm. 21, p. 160, lines 7-9.

[19] Aristotle, *De Anima* II, 2, 413b 25.

[20] Averroes, *In de Anima* II, comm. 21, pp. 160-161, lines 25-31.

[21] Aristotle, *De Anima* II, 2, 413b 25-26.

[22] Averroes, *In de Anima II*, comm. 21, pp. 160-161, lines 28-31.

parts of the soul, so that they [the eternal and the corruptible] may not come together into one substance of soul.

#9. And that it must be understood in this way is evident from the following: "As for the remaining parts of the soul, it is clear from what has been said that they are not separable,"[23] that is, either with regard to subject or to location. For this was the question put above, and this is what was proved from what was said above. And that it is not to be understood to concern separability from the body, but separability of the powers from one another, is clear from what follows: "That they are different in definition," that is different from one another, "is clear. For the sensitive is different from the opiniona-tive."[24] And thus what is here determined clearly answers the question put above. For the question above was whether one part of the soul is distinct from another part only by reason, or also separate in loca-tion. Having here dismissed that question with regard to the intellect, about which he settles nothing here, he says concerning the other parts of the soul that clearly they are not separable, that is in location, but they are distinct by reason.

#10. With this point secured, that the soul is specified by the vegetative, sensitive, intellective, and motive [powers], he wishes to show next that as regards all those parts, the soul is united to the body not as a sailor to a ship, but as form. And thus, what the common mean-ing of soul is, which had been treated above only in a general way, will have been established.[25]

Now he proves this through the operations of the soul as follows: it is certainly clear that that by which something first operates is the form of the thing operating, just as we are said to know by the soul, and to know by knowledge, but by knowledge first rather than by the soul, because we do not know through the soul except inasmuch as it has knowledge; just as in a similar case we are said to be healed both by reason of the body and of health, but first because of health. And so it is clear that knowledge is the form of the soul as health is of the body.[26]

#11. From this he develops his argument as follows: "The soul is the first principle by which we live (this he says because of the vege-tative power), by which we sense (because of the sensitive power), by which we are moved (because of the motive power), and by which we understand (because of the intellective power); and he concludes: "Wherefore the soul will undoubtedly be a certain definable form and

[23] Aristotle, *De Anima* II, 2, 413b 27-29. See also #7 of *De Unitate Intel-lectus* and *Comm. in de Anima* III, lect. 7, 673.

[24] Aristotle, *De Anima* II, 2, 413b 29-30. See also St. Thomas, *Comm. in de Anima* II, lect. 4, 269.

[25] See St. Thomas, *Comm. in de Anima* II, lect. 4, 271.

[26] Aristotle, *De Anima* II, 2, 414a 4-13.

species, but not as matter and as subject."[27] Clearly therefore, that which he had said above, that the soul is the act of a physical body, he here concludes not only of the vegetative, sensitive and motive [powers], but also of the intellective [power]. Therefore what Aristotle meant was that that by which we understand is the form of a physical body.

But lest anyone say that that by which we understand does not mean here the possible intellect, but something different, clearly this is excluded by what Aristotle says in III *De Anima*, when speaking of the possible intellect: "I speak moreover of the intellect by which the soul thinks and understands."[28]

(#12-16. Aristotle states that the intellect is a power of the
soul which is the form of the body.—Words at the
beginning of III *De Anima*.)

#12. But before we take up the words of Aristotle which are in III *De Anima*, we should dwell still further on his words in II *De Anima*, so that from a comparison of his words with each other, it may be clear what his teaching on the soul was. For when he had defined the soul in general, he begins to distinguish its powers; and he says that "the powers of the soul are vegetative, sensitive, appetitive, locomotive, intellective."[29] And that the intellective [power] is the intellect is clear through what he adds later, when he explains the division: "But for other beings, the intellective and intellect, as in men."[30] He therefore means that the intellect is a power of the soul, which is the act of the body.

#13. And that he had said that the intellect is a power of this soul and that the definition of the soul stated above is common to all the parts mentioned before is evident from his conclusion: "Therefore it is clear, since there will undoubtedly be one definition of soul in the same way as there is one of figure; for the figure is not there as something over and beyond the triangle and the others that follow from it; nor is the soul here as something over and beyond the parts mentioned."[31] Therefore we should not seek for another soul over and beyond those already mentioned, to which the above-mentioned definition of the soul is common.

Aristotle makes no further mention of the intellect in Book II, except his later remark that "the last and the least (he says) is reason-

[27] *Ibid.*, 414a 12-14.
[28] *Ibid.*, III, 4, 429a 23.
[29] *Ibid.*, II, 3, 414a 30-31.
[30] *Ibid.*, 414b 18-20.

[31] *Ibid.*, 414b 20-24. And see St. Thomas, *Comm. in de Anima* II, lect. 5, 295.

ing and intellect,"[32] because, namely, it is in fewer beings, as is clear from what follows.

#14. But because there is a great difference as regards the mode of operation, between the intellect and the imagination, he adds that "the notion of the speculative intellect is different."[33] For he reserves this inquiry for Book III. And lest anyone should say, as Averroes wrongly explains,[34] that the reason Aristotle says that the notion of the speculative intellect is different is that the intellect is neither the soul nor a part of the soul, he immediately excludes this at the beginning of Book III,[35] where he takes up again the treatment of the intellect. For he says: "As for the part of the soul by which the soul knows and understands."[36]

Nor should anyone say that this may be said only about the possible intellect, as distinguished from the agent intellect, as some foolishly say.[37] For this was said before Aristotle proves that there is a possible and agent intellect; whence he here speaks of that part as intellect in general, insofar as it includes both agent and possible intellect, as he has previously in Book II clearly distinguished the intellect from the other parts of the soul, as has already been said.[38]

#15. Moreover, the wonderful carefulness and order in Aristotle's procedure must be considered.[39] For he next begins in Book III to treat those things concerning the intellect which he had left unsettled in Book II.

Now he had previously left two things unsettled about the intellect. First, whether the intellect is separated from the other parts of the soul only by reason, or also in location; this he had left unsettled when he said: "Nothing is as yet evident concerning the intellect and perceiving power."[40] And this question he first takes up again when he says: "Whether by something existing separable (namely from other parts of the soul), or not separable according to size, but only according

---

[32] Aristotle, *De Anima* II, 3, 414b 18-20.

[33] *Ibid.*, 415a 11-12.

[34] Averroes, *In de Anima* II, comm. 32, p. 178, lines 32-37.

[35] Keeler here notes that although in *Comm. in de Anima* St. Thomas follows the division of books as they are in the Greek copies, in this work (because he is concerned with Averroes and the Averroists), he uses the division which the Arabs used, according to which Book III begins with Chapter 4 of Book III of the Greek (429a 10).

[36] Aristotle, *De Anima* III, 4, 429a 10-11.

[37] Perhaps a reference to Averroes, *In de Anima* III, comm. 4, p. 385, lines 58-59.

[38] See *De Unitate Intellectus*, #8.

[39] Here Keeler remarks that the carefulness and order attributed to the Philosopher is perhaps a little overrated, but he adds that this is a natural and just interpretation of the text of 429a 10-13 with which it is directly concerned.

[40] Aristotle, *De Anima* II, 2, 413b 24-25. See *De Unitate Intellectus*, #7.

to reason."[41] His meaning here of "separable according to size" is the same as what he had spoken of above as "separable in location."

#16. Secondly, he had left unsettled the difference between the intellect and the other parts of the soul, when he said afterwards: "But the notion of the speculative intellect is different."[42] And this he at once inquires into when he says: "We must consider what the difference is."[43] For he intends to assign such a difference as can stand with either of the premises, namely whether it [the intellect] is separable in size or location from the other parts, or not. The very manner of speaking makes this sufficiently clear. For he says that it should be considered what the intellect's difference from the other parts of the soul is, whether it is separable from them in size or location, that is in subject, or not separable in that way but only by reason.[44] Whence it is clear that he does not intend to show such a difference as this: that it is a substance separate in its being from the body (for this could not stand with both of the premises); but he intends to assign a difference with respect to its way of acting; whence he adds: "And how indeed does the very act of understanding come about?"[45]

So, therefore, from what we can understand of Aristotle's words thus far, it is clear that he meant the intellect to be a part of the soul which is the act of a physical body.

(#17-26. The intellect is compared with sense. Empedocles and Anaxagoras.)

#17. But because in certain words that follow, the Averroists wished to understand Aristotle's meaning to have been that the intellect is not the soul which is the act of the body, or part of such a soul;[46] for that reason his next words must be considered even more attentively.

Immediately therefore after the question proposed about the difference between the intellect and sense, he asks[47] in what respect intellect is like sense and in what respect it is different from it. For he had pre-

[41] *Ibid.*, III, 4, 429a 11-12.
[42] *Ibid.*, II, 3, 415a 11-12. See *De Un. Int.*, #14.
[43] *Ibid.*, III, 4, 429a 12.
[44] *Ibid.*, 429a 11-12.
[45] *Ibid.*, 429a 13.
[46] See Averroes, *In de Anima* II, comm. 21, p. 160, lines 6-15; comm. 22, p. 161, lines 8-16. Siger of Brabant is reported by John Baconthorp to have said that if by intellect we mean the immaterial possible intellect that we call the intellective soul in us, then the Philosopher does not prove that the intellective soul is the form of man. —John of Baconthorp, *Quodlibeta* (Venice, 1527), fol. 2vb. See M. Chossat, "St. Thomas d'Aquin et Siger de Brabant," in *Revue de Philosophie* 24 (1914), pp. 558-563.
[47] See also St. Thomas, *Comm. in de Anima* III, lect. 7.

viously settled two things[48] about sense, namely that sense is in potency to sensible things, and that sense suffers from and is injured by the excessive intensities of sensible things. This therefore is what Aristotle is trying to point out when he says: "If therefore understanding is like sensing, either it will surely suffer from an intelligible object," inasmuch as intellect would be injured by an excessively intense intelligible object as sense by an excessively intense sensible, "or something of this kind, yet different."[49] That is: or understanding is something like this, that is like sensing, but different in this respect that it is not passible.

#18. To this question therefore he immediately answers; and he concludes (not from what precedes but from what follows, although what follows is clear from what precedes) that this part of the soul "must be impassible"[50] so that it is not injured, as is sense. (It has however another kind of passivity, inasmuch as understanding is said in a general way to suffer.) In this respect, therefore, it differs from sense.

But next he shows how it is like sense, because, namely, a part of this kind must be "receptive of an intelligible species," and be "in potency" to a species of this kind, and "not be this" in act according to its own nature;[51] just as it was previously said about sense, that it is in potency to sensible things, and not in act.[52] And from this he concludes that it must be that "the intellect is related to intelligible things as sense is related to sensible things."[53]

#19. But this led to the exclusion of the opinion of Empedocles and other ancient thinkers who stated that the knower is of the nature of the thing known, for example that we know earth inasmuch as we are earth, and water inasmuch as we are water.[54] But Aristotle showed above that this is not true of sense because a sense power is not actually but potentially those things that it senses; and here he says the same thing of the intellect.

But there is a difference between sense and intellect, because a sense is not able to know all things, but sight can know only colors; hearing, only sounds; and so for the rest; whereas the intellect is able to know all things without such limitations. Now the ancient philosophers used to say, since they were of the opinion that the knower must have the nature of the thing known, that the soul, in order to know all things, must be a mixture of the principles of all things. But because Aristotle already proved through a comparison with sense, that the intellect is not actually but only potentially that which it knows, he concluded to the contrary that "because the intellect knows all things,

---

[48] Aristotle, *De Anima* II, 11, 423b 30 - 424al; 424a 25 -b3.
[49] *Ibid.*, III, 4, 429a 13-15.
[50] *Ibid.*, 429a 15.
[51] *Ibid.*, 429a 15-16.
[52] *Ibid.*, II, 5, 417a 6-7.
[53] *Ibid.*, III, 4, 429a 17-18.
[54] *Ibid.*, I, 2, 404b 13-15. H. Diels, *Die Fragmente der Vorsokratiker*, fr. 109.

it must be unmixed,"[55] that is, not composed of all things as Empedocles had stated.

#20. And to show this, he brings in the testimony of Anaxagoras,[56] who was not, however, speaking about this same intellect, but about the intellect that moves all things. Therefore just as Anaxagoras said that that intellect was unmixed, so that it might rule by moving and separating out, so we can say about the human intellect that it must be unmixed so that it may know all things; and this he proves thereafter and so the following line is found in the Greek: "That which appears within will hinder and obstruct what is without."[57] This can be understood from something similar in sight;[58] for if there were some color within the pupil, that inside color would make it impossible for an outside color to be seen and in some way would prevent the eye from seeing other things.

#21. Likewise, if the nature of the things which the intellect knows, for example, earth or water, what is hot or cold, or anything of this kind, were intrinsic to the intellect, that nature within the intellect would hinder and in some way prevent the intellect from knowing other things. Because therefore it knows all things, he concludes[59] that "it cannot itself have any nature" which is determined by the sensible natures that it knows; "but it has this nature alone, that it is possible," that is, in potency to those things that it knows, so far as its own nature is concerned; but it becomes those things in act during the time in which it actually knows them; as the sense in act becomes the sensible in act, as he had said above in Book II.[60] He therefore concludes that the intellect "before it understands (in act), is actually none of those existing things."[61] This is contrary to what the ancient thinkers said, namely that it is actually all things.

#22. And because he had mentioned the statement of Anaxagoras, who speaks about the intellect that rules all things, so that it would not be supposed that his own conclusion concerned that intellect, he uses the following manner of speaking: "Therefore the intellect that is said of the soul—and I mean the intellect by which the soul thinks and understands—is in no respect in act,"[62] etc. From this two things are clear: First, that he is not speaking here of an intellect which is a separate substance, but of the intellect which he had said above[63]

---

[55] Aristotle, *De Anima*, III, 4, 429a 18-20.

[56] *Ibid.*, 429a 19-24. See also I, 2, 405 a 15-19, and *Met.* I, 8, 989a 30-989b 20; Diels, *op. cit.*, fr. 12.

[57] *Ibid.*, III, 4, 429a 20-21.

[58] See St. Thomas, *Comm. in de Anima* III, lect. 7, 680.

[59] Aristotle, *De Anima* III, 4, 429a 21-22.

[60] *Ibid.*, III, 2, 425b 27-28; II, 5, 418a 3-6; II, 11, 423b 30-424a 1.

[61] *Ibid.*, III, 4, 429a 22-24.

[62] *Ibid.*

[63] See *De Un. Int.*, #12-14.

was a power and part of the soul, by which the soul understands. Secondly, that which he proved through what was said above, that is, that the intellect does not have a nature that is in act.

#23. But he has not yet proved that it is not a power in the body, as Averroes says;[64] but he immediately concludes this from the preceding; for this follows: "Wherefore it is not reasonable to suppose that it is mixed with a body."[65] And this second point he proves through the first which he had proved above, namely, that the intellect does not have in act any of the natures of sensible things. From this it is clear that it is not mixed with a body, because if it were mixed with a body, it would have some of the corporeal natures. And this is what he adds: "For an intellect would surely become of some kind, either hot or cold, if it were to have an organ like a sense faculty."[66] For the sense is proportioned to its organ and in some way is assimilated to its nature. Therefore the operation of the sense is changed even according to the change of the organ. This therefore is the meaning of the expression, "not to be mixed with body," that intellect does not have an organ as the sense does.

#24. And that the intellect of the soul does not have an organ, he shows[67] by the remark "of certain men who said that the soul is the place of species," taking "place" in its broad meaning as anything receptive, in the manner of the Platonists; except that to be the place of species does not pertain to the whole soul, but only to the intellective [power]. For the sensitive part does not receive the species in itself but in its organ; whereas the intellective part does not receive them in an organ, but in itself. Besides, the intellect is not the place of species in such a way that it has them in act, but only in potency. Since, therefore, he has now shown what pertains to the intellect from its likeness with sense, he comes back to his first statement, that is, that "the intellective part must be impassible,"[68] and so by a wondrous subtlety, from its very similarity with sense, he concludes its dissimilarity. He therefore shows subsequently "that sense and intellect are not impassible in the same way,"[69] inasmuch as sense is injured by an excessively intense sensible, but the intellect is not injured by an excessively intense intelligible. And from what has already been proved, he states as the cause of this, "that the sense [power] does not exist without a body, but the intellect is separate."[70]

[64] Averroes, *In de Anima* III, 4, p. 383, lines 6-10.

[65] Aristotle, *De Anima* III, 4, 429a 24-25.

[66] *Ibid.*, 429a 25-26. See *Comm. in de Anima* III, lect. 7, 684.

[67] Aristotle, *De Anima* III, 4, 429a 27-

29. See also *Physics* IV, 2, 209b 11-17; Plato, *Timaeus*, 52 B.

[68] Aristotle, *De Anima* III, 4, 429a 14-15.

[69] *Ibid.*, 429a 29 - 429b 5.

[70] *Ibid.*, 429b 3-4.

#25. Now it is especially this last word that they take over to support their error, intending by this to hold that the intellect is neither the soul nor a part of the soul, but some separate substance.[71] But they quickly forget what Aristotle said just prior to this. For he says here that "the sense power does not exist without a body, and the intellect is separate," as he said above that the intellect "would become of some kind, either hot or cold, if it were to have an organ like a sense faculty."[72] Therefore, the reason he says that the sense [power] does not exist without a body, whereas the intellect is separate, is that the sense has an organ whereas the intellect does not.[73]

#26. Most clearly therefore it appears without any doubt, from the words of Aristotle that this was his position about the possible intellect, namely that the intellect is something belonging to the soul which is the act of the body; but in such a way that the intellect of the soul does not have a corporeal organ as the other powers of the soul have.

(#27-30. The interpretation stated above is confirmed by *Physics* II, 2.)

#27. Now how it is possible that the soul is the form of the body and some power of the soul is not a power of the body, is not hard to understand if one would consider [the point] in other things as well. For we see in many instances that a form is indeed the act of a body made of a mixture of elements, and yet it has some power which is not the power of any element, but which belongs to such a form by reason of a higher principle, for example, a celestial body; just as a magnet has the power of attracting iron, and jasper of checking the blood flow.[74] And gradually we see that the more noble the forms, the more they have powers that transcend matter. Whence the highest of the forms, which is the human soul, has a power totally transcending corporeal matter, namely the intellect.[75] So therefore the intellect is separate because it is not a power in the body, but is a power in the soul; moreover, the soul is the act of the body.

#28. Nor do we say that the soul in which the intellect is, so exceeds corporeal matter that it does not have its being in the body; but that the intellect, which Aristotle calls a power of the soul, is not the

---

[71] Averroes, *In de Anima* II, comm. 21 & 22, pp. 160-161. See view attributed to Siger by John of Baconthorp, *Quodlibeta* I, 1, fol. 3rb.

[72] Aristotle, *De Anima* III, 4, 429a 25-26.

[73] See St. Thomas, *In de Anima* III, lect. 7, 699.

[74] See St. Thomas, *Quaestiones Disputatae de Anima*, 1; *De Spir. Creat.*, 2. St. Albert says of jasper that it stops the flow of blood: *De Mineralibus*, Lib. II, tract. II, cap. VIII, in *Opera Omnia*, vol. 5 (Paris: Vives, 1890), p. 39.

[75] St. Thomas, *Q.D. de Anima*, 2.

act of the body. For the soul is not the act of the body through the mediation of its powers, but the soul through its own self is the act of the body, giving specific being to the body. Some of its powers, however, are acts of certain parts of the body, perfecting them [the parts] for some operations. On the other hand, such a power as the intellect is the act of no body, because its operation is not accomplished through a corporeal organ.

#29. And lest it seem to anyone that we are saying this from our own interpretation and beyond Aristotle's meaning, we should quote the words of Aristotle saying this expressly. For he asks in Book II of the *Physics:* "How far must (a physicist) know the species and essence?"[76] For it is not the work of a physicist to consider every form. And he solves the question by adding: "To what extent does a doctor know a nerve, or an artisan know bronze?"[77] that is, to some end. And he shows to what end by adding: "until he knows the purpose of each."[78] It is as if he were saying: a doctor considers a nerve insofar as it pertains to health, for health is the reason why a doctor considers a nerve; and likewise an artisan considers bronze, on account of his art. And because a physicist considers form insofar as it is in matter (for such is the form of a movable body), in a similar way it must be understood that the natural philosopher considers form in so far as it is in matter.

#30. The end therefore of the physicist's consideration of forms, is in the forms which are in a certain way in matter, and in another way not in matter. For such forms are on the boundary of separate and material forms.[79] Whence he adds: "and to these which are indeed separated species, but in matter, the natural philosopher's consideration of forms is limited."[80] Now what these forms are he shows, adding: "For man and the sun generate man from matter."[81]

The form of man therefore is in matter, and is separate: in matter indeed, according to the being that it gives to the body for so it is the term of generation,[82] but separate according to the power which is proper to man, namely according to the intellect. It is therefore not impossible that some form be in matter, and its power be separate, as has been explained concerning the intellect.

[76] Aristotle, *Physics* II, 2, 194b 10-11.
[77] *Ibid.*, 194b 11-12.
[78] *Ibid.*, 194b 12.
[79] See St. Thomas, *Sum. Theol.* I, q 77, a. 2; *Liber de Causis* 2 (ed. Bardenhewer), p. 165.
[80] Aristotle, *Phys.* II, 2, 194b 12-13.
[81] *Ibid.*, 194b 13-14. Keeler points out that according to Aristotle, all generation and corruption depends on the annual motion of the sun, in so far as it draws near and recedes. See *On Generation and Corruption* II, c. 10.
[82] See *In octo libros Physicorum Expositio* II, lect. 4; *Sum. Theol.* I, q. 76, a. 1, ad 1.

(#31-43. Reply to someone arguing that the intellect is incorruptible according to the Philosopher, and therefore not the form of a corruptible body.)

#31. But in still another way they proceed to show that it was Aristotle's teaching that the intellect is not the soul, or part of the soul that is united to the body as its form. For Aristotle says in several places that the intellect is eternal and incorruptible, as is clear in Book II of the *De Anima*, where he said: "It belongs to this alone to be separated as the eternal from the corruptible;"[83] and in Book I, where he said that "the intellect seems to be some kind of substance and is not corrupted;"[84] and in Book III where he said: "Only when separated is it what it truly is, and this alone is immortal and eternal,"[85] (although this last [statement] certain men explain as concerning not the possible intellect, but the agent intellect). From all these words it is clear that Aristotle meant that the intellect is incorruptible.

#32. But it seems that nothing incorruptible can be the form of a corruptible body. For it is not accidental to form, but it is proper to it of itself that it be in matter; otherwise only an accidental union would result from matter and form. Now nothing can exist without that which properly inheres in it. Therefore the form of a body cannot be without a body. If therefore a body be corruptible, it follows that the form of a body is corruptible.

Besides, the forms which are separate from matter and the forms which are in matter are not the same in species, as is proved in Book VII of the *Metaphysics*.[86] Much less therefore can a form that is numerically one and the same, at one time be in the body, yet at another time be without the body. Therefore when the body is destroyed, either the form of the body is destroyed, or it goes into another body. If therefore the intellect is the form of the body, it seems to follow necessarily that the intellect is corruptible.

#33. Now it should be noted that this reasoning influenced the Platonists. For Gregory of Nyssa[87] imputes to Aristotle an opposite

[83] Aristotle, *De Anima* II, 2, 413b 25-26.
[84] *Ibid.*, I, 4, 408b 17-18.
[85] *Ibid.*, III, 5 ,430a 22-23. In #36 St. Thomas comments directly on the interpretation of this line.
[86] Aristotle, *Met.* VII, 11, 1036b 22-24, 1037a 1-2; 16, 1040b 28 - 1041a4.
[87] Nemesius of Emessa, *De Natura Hominis*, c. 2 (PG 40, 571 B) and/ or PG 45, 205 A). Keeler notes that all citations of Gregory of Nyssa are taken from Chapters 2 & 3 of a work of Nemesius of Emessa. *De Natura Hominis* (PG 40, 503-818), a work which was also included by Migne among the works of Gregory of Nyssa under the title, *De Anima* (PG 45, 187-222). For an account of how the work of Nemesius was attributed to Gregory in the Middle Ages, Keeler refers the reader to the article by E. Amann, "Nemesius," in *Dictionnaire de Théologie Catholique*, Tome 11, col. 65-66.

conclusion: that because Aristotle held that the soul is form, he held that it is corruptible. On account of this [reasoning] some men in fact held that the soul goes from body to body. Some have even held that the soul would have some kind of incorruptible body from which it would never be separated.[88] And therefore, it must be shown from Aristotle's words that he held the intellective soul to be form in such a manner that he nevertheless held it to be incorruptible.

#34. For in Book XI of the *Metaphysics*, after he had shown that forms do not exist prior to matter, "since when a man is cured, then health exists, and the shape of a bronze sphere exists together with the bronze sphere;"[89] he next asks whether any form remains after the matter, and he says yes, according to the translation of Boethius: "Whether indeed, there remains something afterwards (that is, after the matter), must be considered. For in certain cases nothing would prevent this, as for example if the soul is of this kind, not all the soul, but the intellect, for perhaps it is impossible for all the soul."[90] It is clear, therefore, that he says that nothing hinders the soul which is a form from remaining after the body so far as its intellective part is concerned, although it did not exist before the body. For since he had said absolutely that "moving causes are prior, but not formal causes,"[91] his question was not whether any form was prior to matter, but whether any form may remain after matter; and he says that nothing prevents this with respect to a form which is the soul, so far as its intellective part is concerned.

#35. Since therefore, according to the foregoing words of Aristotle, this form which is the soul may remain after the body, not the whole soul, but the intellect, it should be considered why the soul remains

[88] Keeler notes that some of the ancient neoplatonists (esp. Proclus) admitted some such thing, and that St. Thomas usually refers to this doctrine as "Platonic" without naming any author, as in *Sum. Theol.* I, q. 76, a. 7. See Proclus, *Elements of Theology*, prop. 196; St. Augustine, *City of God* X, 30.

[89] Aristotle, *Met.* XII, 3, 1070a 22-24.

[90] *Ibid.*, 1070a 24-27. Keeler notes that the reference is to an old version taken from the Greek, but hardly from Boethius, and that Book XII is cited as XI. He refers to M. Grabmann, *Forschungen über die lateinischen Aristoteles übersetzungen des XIII Jahrhunderts, Beiträge* XVII, 5-6 (Münster, 1916); F. Pelster, *Die Griechisch-lateinischen Metaphysik-übersetzungen des Mittelalters, Beiträge*, Supplementband II (Münster, 1923), pp. 89-118; Pelster, "Die Übersetzungen der aristotelischen Metaphysik in den Werken des hl. Thomas von Aquin," in *Gregorianum* III, 16 (1935) 325-348, 541-561; A. Dondaine, *Bulletin Thomiste* (1933) pp. 199-213. See also D. Salman, O.P., who notes that Book XI (K) was missing from the translations of Aristotle's *Metaphysics* that were known to St. Thomas through 1270. See Salman, "Saint Thomas et les traductions latines des Métaphysiques d'Aristote,' *Archives d'-Histoire Doctrinale et Littéraire du Moyen Âge* VII (Paris: Vrin, 1933) pp. 106, 120.

[91] Aristotle, *Met.* XII, 3, 1070a 21-22.

after the body when other forms do not remain after their matter; and why the soul remains according to its intellective part, and not according to its other parts. Indeed, it is necessary to take the explanation of this from the very words of Aristotle. For he says: "But only when separated is it what it truly is, and this alone is immortal and eternal."[92] Therefore, he seems to give the following explanation for his position that this alone seems to be immortal and eternal:—because this alone is separate.

#36. But there can be a doubt concerning what he is talking about in this text. Some say[93] he is talking about the possible intellect; some say that it is about the agent intellect. Each of these seems to be false if the words of Aristotle are carefully considered. For Aristotle had said of each [the agent and the possible intellect] that it is separate. Therefore it must be understood of the whole intellective part, which indeed is called separate because it has no organ, as is clear from the words of Aristotle.

#37. Now Aristotle had said in the beginning of the book, *De Anima*, that "if there is some work or passion proper to the soul, then the soul can certainly be separated; but if there is none proper to it, it certainly will not be separable."[94] The reasoning leading to this conclusion is as follows: since each thing operates insofar as it is a being, to operate belongs to each thing in the same way as to be belongs to it. The forms, therefore, which have no operation without being joined with their matter, do not themselves operate, but it is the composite that operates through the form. Whence indeed, forms of this kind do not themselves, properly speaking exist, but by means of them something exists. For just as it is not heat, but a hot thing, that heats; so also heat is not properly said to exist, but a hot thing exists through heat. On account of this Aristotle says in Book XI of the *Metaphysics* that it is not truly said of accidents that they are beings, but rather that they are of being.[95]

#38. And the reasoning is similar with respect to substantial forms which have no operation without being joined to matter, with this exception that forms of this kind are the principle of being substantially. The form, therefore, which has an operation according to some potency or power of its own apart from being joined with its matter, is that which itself has being, nor does it exist only through the being

[92] Aristotle, *De Anima* III, 5, 430a 22-23.

[93] See Averroes, *In de Anima* III, comm. 20, pp. 443-454, for Averroes' interpretation of this line, together with Averroes' report of the interpretations of Alexander and Themistius.

[94] Aristotle, *De Anima* I, 1, 403a 10-12.

[95] Aristotle, *Met.* XII, 1, 1069a 21-22; VII, 1, 1028a 18-20. See St. Thomas, *Comm. in Met.* XII, lect. 1, 2419. On the use of XI rather than XII in referring to Aristotle's *Met.*, see references in note 90.

of the composite, like other forms, but rather the composite exists through its [the form's] being. And, therefore, when the composite is destroyed, there is destroyed that form which exists through the being of the composite, whereas there is no need that, upon the destruction of the composite, there be destroyed that form through whose being the composite exists and which does not itself exist through the being of the composite.

#39. But someone might bring as an objection against this, what Aristotle says in Book I of the *De Anima*, that "to understand and to love and to hate are not passions of that (that is, of the soul), but of the one having that insofar as he has that; wherefore when this (composite) is corrupted, it [the soul] neither remembers nor loves, for these activities did not belong to that [the soul], but to the composite which has been destroyed."[96] But the answer is clear through the remark Themistius makes when he explains this by saying: Aristotle "now is more like one who is doubting than one who is teaching."[97] For he had not yet destroyed the teaching of those who say that intellect and sense are not different.

#40. Whence in that whole chapter he speaks of intellect as he speaks of sense. This is especially evident where he proves that the intellect is incorruptible by means of the example of sense, which is not corrupted by old age. Wherefore, through the whole chapter, he speaks conditionally and with doubt as an inquirer, always joining those things which pertain to the intellect to those which pertain to the sense; this is especially clear from what he says in the beginning of the solution: "For if and most especially, to feel pain and to be glad and to understand" etc.[98] But if anyone stubbornly wishes to say that Aristotle is speaking there in a definitive way, the answer still remains, because to understand is said to be the act of the composite not *per se* but *per accidens,* inasmuch as the object of the act, that is, the phantasm, is in a bodily organ; not that that act is exercised *through* a bodily organ.

#41. Now if anyone should ask further: if the intellect does not understand without a phantasm, how then will the soul have an intellectual operation, after it has been separated from the body? the one who makes this objection ought, however, to know that the solution of this question does not pertain to natural philosophy. Whence Aristotle, in speaking of the soul in Book II of the *Physics,* says: "But it is the work of first philosophy to determine how this separable thing

[96] Aristotle, *De Anima* I, 4, 408b 25-29.
[97] Themistius, *Paraphrasis eorum quae de Anima Aristotelis* II, lines 90-91, p. 75, in *Commentaire sur le Traité de l'Âme d'Aristote: Traduction de* *Guillaume de Moerbeke,* ed. G. Verbeke (Louvain: Publications Universitaires de Louvain, 1957).
[98] Aristotle, *De Anima* I, 4, 408b 5-6.

is constituted and what it is."[99] For it must be thought that the separated [soul] will have a different mode of understanding from that which the conjoined [soul] has, that is, one like that of other separate substances. Whence it is not without cause that Aristotle asks in Book III of the *De Anima* "whether the intellect that is not separate from a body may know something separate."[100] By this he gives us to understand that when it has been separated, the intellect will be able to know something that it could not know while it is not separate.

#42. In these words it must also be carefully noted that, although he had said above that both intellects (i.e. agent and possible) are separate, yet here he says that they are not separate. For intellect is separate, inasmuch as it is not the act of an organ; but it is not separate inasmuch as it is a part or power of the soul which is the act of the body, as was said above. But from what he says in the beginning of Book XII of the *Metaphysics*[101] (and I have seen 10 of these books, though not yet translated into our language), it can most certainly be concluded that Aristotle solved questions of this kind in what he evidently wrote concerning separate substances.

#43. According to this, therefore, it is clear that arguments brought forth to the contrary[102] do not demonstrate with necessity. For it is essential to a soul that it be united to a body, but this is hindered accidentally, not because of the soul, but because of the body which is corrupted. Just as it belongs essentially to a light thing to be up, and "this is the to be for a light thing, that it be up," as Aristotle says in

[99] Aristotle, *Phys.* II, 2, 194b 14-15.
[100] Aristotle, *De Anima* III, 7, 431b 17-19.
[101] Aristotle, *Met.* XIII, 1, 1076a 10-13. This is the reference that Keeler gives. He says that St. Thomas calls this Book XII (rather than XIII) because of the missing Book XI. (See note 90) However, Salman would rather give the reference as *Met.* VII, 2, 1028b 13-16; the "XII" in his opinion was a paleographical misreading of "VII". See "Saint Thomas et les traductions latines des Métaphysiques d'Aristote," *Archives d'Histoire . . .* VII (1933), p. 97.

The reference to the "10 books" should read, according to Salman, "14 books," as given in the Mandonnet edition of the Opuscula, I, p. 65 (Paris: Lethielleux, 1927). Although Pelster, *Die Griechischlateinischen Metaphysikübersetzungen des M-A., Beiträge* (1923), p.

111, had tentatively suggested that St. Thomas might have been thinking of the apocryphal work, *The Theology of Aristotle,* which consists of ten sections, Salman rejects this theory and says that St. Thomas was rather referring to the parts of the *Metaphysics* he had not yet read. St. Thomas had seen a complete Greek text of Aristotle's *Metaphysics* before November, 1268, but prior to the end of 1270 he did not have the last two books: XIII (M) and XIV (N), or Book XI (K) available in Latin translation. See Salman, *op. cit.,* pp. 92-97, 114, 120.

What St. Thomas says in the last sentence of *De Un. Int.,* #42, he also refers to in #118; in *De Veritate,* q. 18, a. 5, ad 8; *In de Sensu* lect. 1, n. 4; *Q.D.de Anima* 16; *In de Anima* III, lect. 12, 785.
[102] See *De Un. Int.,* #32.

Book VIII of the *Physics;*[103] "yet it may happen through some hindrance that it is not up."

From this the solution of the other issue is also clear. For that which has the nature of being up and that which does not have the nature of being up differ in species; and yet that which has the nature of being up is the same in species and number although sometimes it is up and sometimes, on account of some hindrance, it is not up. So similarly, two forms, one of which has the nature of being united to a body, but the other does not have such a nature, differ in species; but yet something having the nature of being united to the body can be one and the same in species and number, although sometimes it is actually united and sometimes, on account of some hindrance, it is not actually united.

(#44-50. Three other objections to the Philosopher's words are declared invalid.)

#44. But they still take up for the support of their error what Aristotle says in the book, *On the Generation of Animals,* that is, "the intellect alone comes from without and it alone is divine."[104] But no form which is the act of matter comes from without; rather it is educed from the potency of matter. Therefore, the intellect is not the form of the body.

They also object that every form of a mixed body is caused from the elements. Whence, if the intellect were the form of the human body, it would not be from something without, but would be caused from the elements.

They also have an additional objection about this, because it would follow that the vegetative and sensitive [powers] would also be from without. This is contrary to Aristotle, especially if there be one substance of soul whose powers would be vegetative, sensitive, and intellective; for the intellect is from without, according to Aristotle.

#45. Now the solution of these objections readily appears according to what has already been said. For when it is said that every form is educed from the potency of matter, it would seem that we ought to consider what it means that form be educed from the potency of matter. For if it means nothing else than that matter preexists in potency to form, nothing prevents one from saying that in this sense corporeal matter preexists in potency to the intellective soul: whence Aristotle says in the book, *On the Generation of Animals:* "First indeed all [animals] seemed to live thus (namely the separated of foetuses)

---

[103] Aristotle, *Phys.* VIII, 4, 255b 15-20.   [104] Aristotle, *On the Generation of Animals* II, 3, 736b 27-29.

[40]

by the life of a plant. But consequently it is evident that it should be said of the sensitive soul and (of the active) and of the intellective soul; for everything necessarily has potency prior to act."[105]

#46. But because potency is referred to an act, it is necessary that each thing be in potency according to the same nature which is proper to it as being in act. But it has already been shown that it is proper for other forms which have no operation apart from union with matter, to be in act in such a way that they are more properly forms by which the composites exist, and in some way co-existing with the composites, rather than being forms that possess their own being. Whence just as their whole being is in their being joined with matter, so they are said to be totally educed from the potency of matter. But the intellective soul, since it has an operation apart from the body, is not its own being only in its being joined with matter. Whence it cannot be said that it is educed from matter, but rather that it is from an extrinsic principle. And this is clear from the words of Aristotle: "But it remains that intellect alone comes from without, and it alone is divine," and he gives the reason by adding: "For the operation of the body does not at all share in its operation."[106]

#47. But I wonder what is the source of the second objection, namely that if the intellective soul were the form of a mixed body, that it would be caused from a mixture of the elements, since no soul is caused from a mixture of the elements.[107] For Aristotle says immediately after the foregoing words: "Indeed, therefore, every power of the soul is seen to participate in a body that is other and more divine than the named elements; but as one soul differs from another in honor and vileness, so also does such a nature differ. For there exists in the seed of everything that which makes the seeds to be generative, and this is called heat. But this is not fire nor any such power, but is some spirit which is contained in the seed and in the foaming thing. And in this spirit, the nature is proportional to the ordering of the stars."[108] Therefore from a mixture of the elements neither intellect is produced, nor even the vegetative soul.

#48. Now as for the third objection, that it would follow that the vegetative and sensitive [parts] are from without, it is not to the point. For it is already clear from Aristotle's words[109] that he leaves it unsettled whether the intellect differs from the other parts of the soul in subject and location, as Plato said, or only by reason.

[105] *Ibid.,* 736b 12-15.
[106] *Ibid.,* 736b 27-29. See *Sum. Theol.* I, q. 90, a. 2; q. 118, a. 2; *De Potentia Dei* III, 9.
[107] See *Sum. cont. Gent.* II, 62, 63.
[108] Aristotle, *On the Generation of Animals* II, 3, 736b 29 - 737a 1. See *Sum. cont. Gent.* II, 73; *Sum. Theol.* I, q. 118, a. 1, ad 3.
[109] See *De Un. Int.,* #7, 15, 16.

But if it be granted that they are the same in subject (which is closer to the truth), thus far no difficulty results. For Aristotle says in Book II of the *De Anima* that "there is a similarity between figures and the soul. Both in figures and in living things, it is always true that prior things exist potentially in what succeeds them; as a triangle exists in a square, so is the vegetative in the sensitive."[110]

#49. But if that which is the same in subject is also intellective (which he leaves doubtful), it must similarly be said that the vegetative and sensitive are in the intellective, as a triangle and square are in a pentagon. Now a square is indeed a figure that is, without qualification, other in species than a triangle, but not other than the triangle that is potentially in it; just as the figure 4 is not other than the figure 3 that is part of itself, but it is other than the figure 3 that exists apart from it. And if it should happen that diverse figures are produced by diverse agents, of course a triangle existing apart from a square would have another producing cause than the square would have, just as it also has another species; but the triangle that is in the square would have the same producing cause.

#50. So therefore the vegetative [soul] that exists apart from the sensitive, is indeed another species of soul and has another productive cause; yet there is the same productive cause for the sensitive and for the vegetative which is within the sensitive. If therefore it be stated in this way: that the vegetative and sensitive [parts] which are present within the intellective [part], are from the extrinsic cause which is the cause of the intellective part, no difficulty results. For it is not unsuitable that the effect of a superior agent should have a power that the effect of an inferior agent has, plus still more. Whence also the intellective soul, although it be from an external agent, nevertheless has powers which the vegetative and sensitive souls, coming from inferior agents, also possess.

So therefore, from this careful consideration of almost all the statements which Aristotle made about the human intellect, it is clear that his position was that the human soul is the act of the body, and that the possible intellect is a part or power of that soul.

---

[110] Aristotle, *De Anima* II, 3, 414b 28-32. See St. Thomas, *In de Anima* II, lect. 5, 298; *Q.D. de Anima* 2, ad 8; *Quaestiones Quodlibetales* I, q. 4, a. 6; *De Spir. Creat.*, a. 3 (where, as editors usually note, a part of the text is incorrect.)

CHAPTER II.

(#51-59. What other Peripatetics thought about the relation of the possible intellect to man.)

(#51-56. The Greeks: Themistius, Theophrastus, Alexander.)

#51. Now we must consider what other Peripatetics thought on this point. And first let us take the words of Themistius in the *Commentary on the Soul*, where he speaks as follows:[1] "That intellect which we say is in potency . . . is more connatural to the soul (i.e., than the agent): But I mean connatural not to every soul, but only to the human soul. And just as light coming to sight and colors in potency, makes sight and colors to be in act, so also that intellect which is in act . . . not only makes the intellect to be in act, but it also makes the intelligibles in potency to be intelligibles in act." And after a few words he concludes: "That relationship which art has to matter, the factive intellect has to that which is in potency. . . . For this reason it is within our power to understand whenever we wish. For art is not of exterior matter . . . but the potency of the whole is clothed by the intellect which is factive; as for example, if the builder were not to exist outside of the wood and the artisan (outside) the brass, they would have the power of penetrating it throughout. In this way, the intellect which is in act, supervening upon the intellect in potency, is made one with it."

#52. And after a few words he concludes:[2] "We therefore are either the intellect which is in potency or the intellect which is in act. If indeed in all things composed of that which is in potency and of that which is in act, to be *this* is one thing and the *to be* of this is another, then I *(ego)* and my to be will be different. And I *(ego)* am the intellect composed of potency and act, but my to be is from that which is in act. Wherefore, both what I think and what I write, the intellect composed of potency and act writes; yet it does not write in so far as it is in potency, but insofar as it is in act; for thence its operation is derived."

And after a few words, still more clearly: "Just as, therefore to be an animal is one thing and the to be of an animal another, yet the

---

[1] Themistius, *Paraphrasis eorum quae de Anima Aristotelis*, in tr. of William of Moerbeke (ed. Verbeke, see note 97) VI, pp. 224-226, lines 1-8, 16-24. Keeler notes that one reason why St. Thomas makes so much of Themistius in the *De Unitate Intellectus* is that in his previous works he had followed the interpretation of Themistius handed down by Averroes. This he considers to be erroneous, now that he has read the version recently translated by William of Moerbeke.

[2] Themistius, *op cit.*, VI, pp. 228-229, lines 67-75, 79-85, 89-91.

to be of an animal is from the soul of the animal; so also I *(ego)* and my to be are different. My to be therefore, is from the soul, but not from every [part of the soul]. My to be is not from the sensitive [part], for this is matter in relation to imagination. Nor again from the imaginative [part], for this is matter in relation to intellect which is in potency. Nor is my to be from that intellect which is in potency for this is matter in relation to the factive intellect. Therefore my to be is from the factive intellect alone." And after a few words he adds: "And nature, having advanced thus far, ceased, as if having nothing else more honorable to which it might subject itself. We accordingly, are the active intellect."

#53. And afterwards, rejecting the opinion of certain men, he says:[3] "Since he (Aristotle) had said that in every nature there is matter and that which moves and perfects matter, it must needs be that these differences also exist in the soul, and that there must be some intellect which is such by becoming all things, and another which is such by making all things. For he says that in the soul there is such an intellect and that it is, as it were, the most honorable part of the human soul." And after a few words he says: "Also from the same text it happens that he confirms what he (Aristotle) thinks, i.e., either that the active intellect is something belonging to us or it is ourselves."

Therefore, it is clear from the foregoing words of Themistius that he says that not only the possible intellect but also the agent [intellect] is part of the human soul, and he asserts that Aristotle thought this; and, further, that man is what he is, not by reason of the sensitive soul, as some falsely say, but from the more principal and intellective part.

#54. I have not indeed seen the books of Theophrastus, but Themistius in his *Commentary,* introduces his words to this effect, saying thus:[4] "Now it is better to set forth the words of Theophrastus both about the intellect in potency and that which is in act. Concerning the one, therefore, which is in potency, he says this: Now how is the intellect existing from without and as if superimposed, and yet connatural? And what is its nature? For indeed it is nothing in act, but it is surely everything in potency, as sense is. For it must not be so understood that it itself does not exist—for this is a point of dispute—but that it is a kind of potency as a subject, as is the case in material things. But this from without, therefore, should be understood not as something added, but as included at the very beginning of generation."

[3] *Ibid.,* VI, pp. 233-234, lines 73-79, 88-90.

[4] *Ibid.,* VI, p. 242, lines 54-62. E. Zeller d i s c u s s e s Theophrastus in *Aristotle and the Earlier Peripatetics,* tr. F. C. Costelloe and J. H. Muirhead (London: Longmans, Green & Co., 1897), Vol. II, 348-416. He cites this passage on p. 393, n. 1.

#55. So therefore, Theophrastus, when he had asked two questions: first, how is the possible intellect from without and yet connatural to us; and secondly, what is the nature of the possible intellect, answers the second question first. (He says that the possible intellect) is in potency to all things, not indeed as being nothing existing, but as sense [is in potency] to sensibles. And from this he draws his answer to the first question, that it is not so understood to be from without as though it were something added accidentally or in some former time, but [is] from the very beginning of generation as though containing and including human nature.

#56. Moreover, that Alexander held that the possible intellect is the form of the body, even Averroes himself admits, although (as I think) he understood the words of Alexander wrongly, just as he had also taken the words of Themistius beyond his meaning. For what he says[5] is that Alexander has said that the possible intellect is nothing other than a preparation which is in human nature, a preparation for the agent intellect and the intelligibles; he [Alexander] understood this preparation to be nothing other than the intellective potency in the soul for intelligibles. And this is the reason he said it is not a power in the body,—because such a potency does not have a corporeal organ; it is not for the reason that Averroes opposes, namely that no preparation is a power in the body.

(#57-58. Arabs: Avicenna, Algazel.)

#57. To pass now from the Greeks to the Arabs: first it is clear that Avicenna held that the intellect is a power of the soul which is the form of the body. For so he says in his book *On the Soul:* "The active intellect (i.e., practical) needs the body and the powers of the body for all its actions. Moreover, the contemplative intellect needs the body and its powers, but not always nor completely. For it is

[5] Averroes, *In de Anima* III, comm. 14, pp. 430-432, lines 77-147. Keeler notes that in *Comm. in Sent.* II, d. 17, q. 2, a. 1, and in *Sum. cont. Gent.* II, 62, St. Thomas followed the exposition of Alexander's doctrine that Averroes had handed down. However, when he later discovered that the genuine opinion of Themistius came much closer to his own Peripateticism than appeared from the writings of the Commentator, he began to suspect that the Commentator had also given a poor interpretation of Alexander. He therefore imposed a Thomistic interpretation upon Alexander. Keeler adds that such an interpretation is erroneous and that the true mind of Alexander is given with sufficient accuracy in the long and laborious exposition of Averroes. (See Théry. *Alexandre d'Aphrodise,* pp. 27-33, 46 sqq.) Keeler concludes by observing that it is remarkable that St. Thomas did not have recourse to the fragment of Alexander, the *De Intellectu* (ed. by Théry, *op. cit.,* pp. 74-82) if he was acquainted with it; he does name this work in his *Q.D. de Anima* 6.

sufficient to itself through itself. Moreover, none of these [powers] is the human soul; but the soul is that which has these powers and, as we shall later make clear, is a solitary substance, i.e. *per se*, which has an aptitude for actions. Some of these actions are not perfected in any way except through instruments and their use; but there are some for which instruments are not necessary in any way."[6] Likewise, in the first part he says that "the human soul is the first perfection of a natural instrumental body, according as there is attributed to it the performance of actions by the choice of deliberation and discovery by meditating, and according as it apprehends universals."[7] But it is true that he later says and proves that the "human soul," according to what is proper to it, i.e. according to its intellective power, "is not so related to the body as its form, nor does it need to have an organ prepared for it."[8]

#58. Next must be added the words of Algazel, who speaks thus: "When the mixture of the elements will have been of a more beautiful and more perfect equality, than which nothing more subtle or more beautiful can be found . . ., then it is made fit to receive from the giver of forms a form more beautiful than other forms, which is the soul of man. Now of this human soul there are two powers: one operative and the other cognitive."[9] This he calls the intellect, as is clear from what follows. And yet he later proves by many arguments, that the operation of the intellect is not accomplished through a corporeal organ.

#59. Now these things we have said first, not as though wishing to reject the above error by the texts of the philosophers; but to show that not only the Latins, whose words some do not relish, but also the Greeks and the Arabs were of this opinion: that the intellect is a part

---

[6] Avicenna, *De Anima* V, c. 1, fol. 22vb (Venice, 1508); pp. 111-112 of *Avicenna's De Anima: A Transcription of the Venice Edition* (1508), by G. P. Klubertanz, S.J. (St. Louis University, 1949). Keeler notes that the text of Avicenna cited by St. Thomas coincides almost completely with that which is found in the Venice, 1508 edition.

[7] Avicenna, *De Anima* I, c. 5, fol. 4vb (Klubertanz, p. 19).

[8] *Ibid.*, II, c. 1, fol. 6va. (Klubertanz, p. 28).

[9] Algazel, *Metaphysica* pars II, tr. IV, c. 5; p. 172 in J. T. Muckle (ed.), *Algazel's Metaphysics* (Toronto: St. Michael's College, 1933).

The work known as the *Metaphysics* of Algazel was a part of

Algazel's *Maqâcid el-falâcifa* (*The Tendencies* or *Intentions of the Philosophers*); its purpose was to give an objective summary of philosophical knowledge held by Alfarabi and Avicenna. Algazel follows this with a sequel, the *Tahafut el-falâcifa* in which he refuted or destroyed some of the positions held by these philosophers. Because the *Tahafut* and the prologue to the *Maqâcid* were unknown to St. Albert and St. Thomas, they took Algazel's summary of Avicenna's philosophy to be a statement of his own position. See Introduction to Averroes' *Destructio Destructionum Philosophiae Algazelis*, ed. B. H. Zedler (Milwaukee: Marquette University Press, 1961), pp. 5-7.

or potency or power of the soul which is the form of the body. Wherefore I wonder from which Peripatetics they boast of having taken this error, unless perchance they are less willing to be right with other Peripatetics than to be wrong with Averroes, who was not so much a Peripatetic as a perverter of Peripatetic philosophy.

Chapter III.

(#60-85. It is proved by reason that the intellect is a power of the soul which is the form of the body.)

(#60-62. Aristotle's argument: That the soul is that by which we first understand.)

#60. Since it has been shown from the words of Aristotle and of others who follow him that the intellect is a power of the soul which is the form of the body, although that power itself which is the intellect is not the act of any organ "since the operation of the body does not at all share in its operation," as Aristotle says,[1] we should inquire by reason what must be thought of this. And because, according to Aristotle's doctrine, it is necessary to consider the principles of acts from the acts, it seems that the first point to be considered is the very act proper to the intellect; and this is understanding.

#61. In this way we can have no argument more sound than that which Aristotle sets forth. He argues thus:" The soul is the first principle by which we live and understand; therefore it is a certain definable form or species"[2] of some body. And he relies on this argument to the extent that he calls it a demonstration; for at the beginning of the chapter he speaks thus: "Not only is it necessary to give a definition for an essence, as many expressions do, but also to show that its cause is in it and to prove it."[3] And he gives an example: just as what a tetragon, i.e. a four-sided figure, is, is proved by discovering the mean proportional line.

#62. Now the strength and the binding force of this demonstration are evident from the fact that whoever wishes to turn aside from this way, must hold something unreasonable. For it is clear that this individual man understands; for we would never raise a question about the intellect unless we understood; and when we do raise a question about the intellect, we do not ask about any other principle than that by which we understand. Wherefore Aristotle says: "Now I mean the intellect by which the soul understands."[4]

Moreover Aristotle concludes thus:[5] that if something is the first

---

[1] Aristotle, *On the Generation of Animals* II, 3, 736b 28-29.

[2] Aristotle, *De Anima* II, 2, 414a 12-14. See St. Thomas, *Sum. cont. Gent.* II, 59.

[3] Aristotle, *De Anima* II, 2, 413a 12-19. See St. Thomas, *In de Anima* II, lect. 3, 248-251; Averroes, *In de Anima* II, comm. 12, pp. 150-151, lines 55-65. Keeler notes, however, that in Aristotle's example (cited in the last line of *De Un. Int.*, #61), Aristotle did not mean a four-sided figure or square but the process of becoming squared, or "squaring."

[4] Aristotle, *De Anima* III, 4, 429a 23.

[5] Keeler says: "Aristotle does not explicitly give this conclusion, and his argument is weakened by the ambiguous wording he introduces concerning the nature of the intellect."

principle by which we understand, that must be the form of the body; since he has already made clear that that by which anything first of all operates is the form. And this is evident through the reason that everything acts in so far as it is in act, but everything is in act through the form. Whence it must be that that by which something first acts is the form.

(#63-66. Averroes' explanation is disproved.)

#63. Now if you should say that the principle of this act of understanding, a principle that we call the intellect, is not the form, you will have to find a way in which the action of that principle may be the action of this man. This some persons have tried to state in different ways.

One of these, Averroes,[6] held that the principle of this kind of understanding, a principle that is called the possible intellect, is not the soul nor a part of the soul, except equivocally, but rather that it is a separate substance. He said[7] that the understanding of that separate substance is my understanding or that person's understanding, in so far as that possible intellect is joined to me or to you through phantasms which are in me and in you. He said that this is accomplished in the following way. Now the intelligible species, which becomes one with the possible intellect since it is its form and act, has two subjects: one, the phantasms themselves; the other, the possible intellect. So therefore the possible intellect is in contact with us through its form by means of the phantasms; and thus, as long as the possible intellect understands, this man understands.

#64. But that this is no explanation is evident for three reasons.

First of all, because such a contact of the intellect with man would not be from the beginning of man's generation, as Theophrastus says[8] and as Aristotle implies in Book II of the *Physics*,[9] where he says that the term of the natural philosopher's consideration of forms is the form according to which man is generated from man and the sun. Now it is clear that the term of the natural philosopher's consideration is the intellect. But according to Averroes' statement, the intellect would not

[6] Averroes, *In de Anima* II, comm. 21, pp. 160-161, lines 25-33; comm. 32, p. 178, lines 33-37; III, comm. 4, pp. 385-386, lines 78-105.

[7] *Ibid.*, III, comm. 5, p. 400, lines 379-394; pp. 411-412, lines 707-728. See St. Thomas, *Sum. cont. Gent.* II, 59; *Q.D. de Anima* 2; *De Spir. Creat.* 2; *Sum. Theol.* I, q. 76, a. 1.

[8] Theophrastus, as quoted by Themi-

stius, *op. cit.* VI, p. 242, lines 54-62. On Theophrastus, see *De Un. Int.*, #54-55. Keeler notes that the same argument is used in *Sum. cont. Gent.* II, 59, and that in *Sum. cont. Gent.* II, 60, St. Thomas refutes the answer that Averroes gave (*In de Anima* III, comm. 5, p. 405, lines 520-527.)

[9] Aristotle, *Phys.* II, 2, 194b 9-14.

be in contact with man according to his generation, but according to the operation of sense, in so far as he is actually sensing. For the imagination "is moved by sense in act," as is said in the book, *De Anima*.[10]

#65. But secondly,[11] because this conjoining would not be accord- to a single principle, but according to diverse principles. For it is clear that the intelligible species, in so far as it is in the phantasm is potentially understood; but it is in the possible intellect in so far as it is actually understood and abstracted from phantasms. If, therefore, the intelligible species is not the form of the possible intellect except in so far as it is abstracted from phantasms, it follows that the possible intellect is not in contact with the phantasms through the intelligible species, but rather it is separated from them.Unless perhaps it be said that the possible intellect is in contact with phantasms as a mirror is in contact with the man whose appearance is reflected in the mirror. But such a contact clearly does not suffice for the contact of the act. For it is clear that the action of the mirror, which is to represent, cannot on this account be attributed to the man. Whence neither can the action of the possible intellect be attributed, on account of the above-mentioned joining, to this man who is Socrates, in such a way that this man would understand.

#66. Thirdly, even if it were granted that a species that is numerically one and the same would be the form of the possible intellect and would at the same time be in the phantasms, such a union would still not suffice to explain that this man would understand. For it is clear that through the intelligible species something is understood, but through the intellective power he understands something;[12] just as also through the sensible species something is sensed, but through the sensitive power he senses something. This is why a wall in which there is color whose sensible species-in-act is in sight, is seen and does not see; but an animal having the power of sight in which there is such a species, does see. Now the aforesaid union of the possible intellect with man, in whom there are phantasms whose species are in the possible intellect, is like the union of the wall in which there is color with the sight in which is the species of its color. Therefore, just as the wall does not see, but its color is seen; so it would follow that man would not understand but that his phantasms would be understood by the pos-

[10] Aristotle, *De Anima* III, 3, 429a 1-2.

[11] Keeler notes that St. Thomas often works out against Averroes the two arguments which follow, sometimes joining them into one (*De Spir. Creat.* 2; *Sum. Theol.* I, q. 76, a. 1); at other times presenting them as more than one (*Sum. cont. Gent.* II, 59; also *In Sent.* II, d. 17, a. 2, a. 1; *Comm. in de Anima* III, lect. 7, 692-694; *Comp. Theol.* 85.)

[12] See St. Thomas, *Q.D. de Anima* 2.

sible intellect. It is therefore impossible, if one follows Averroes' position, to account for the fact that this man understands.

(#67-79. The intellect is not united to the body only as a mover.)

#67. But some who have seen that according to the way of Averroes, it cannot be maintained that this man understands, have turned to another way, and they say that the intellect is united to the body as a mover.[13] Thus, in so far as a unit results from the body and the intellect, as from the mover and thing moved, the intellect is part of this man. Therefore, the operation of the intellect is attributed to this man, just as the operation of the eye, which is to see, is attributed to this man.

But it should be asked of him who holds this, first, what is this singular which is Socrates: Is Socrates the intellect alone, which is a mover? Or is he a thing moved by the intellect, that is a body animated by a vegetative and sensitive soul? Or is he a composite of both? And so far as his position is seen, he would accept this third alternative: that Socrates is something composed of both.

#68. Let us therefore proceed against them by means of the reasoning of Aristotle in Book VIII of the *Metaphysics:*[14] "What is it, therefore, that makes a man one? . . . For of all things which have several parts and are not as it were an aggregate whole but the whole is something besides the parts, there is some reason for the unity of being; as in some things there is touch, in others viscosity, or something else of this kind. . . . But clearly because if they[15] transform [things],

---

[13] Keeler notes that the theory of the intellect mover (to be distinguished from the Platonic doctrine of the soul, as mover of the body) is common to the Arab Peripatetics, at least as far as the agent intellect is concerned; for all of them conceive the relation of the last intelligence to the sublunar world according to the analogy of the relation of higher intelligences to the heavenly sphere belonging to each one. In *Sum. Theol.* I, q. 76, a. 1, St. Thomas refutes the doctrine of intellect as mover.
— On Siger's position, see John of Baconthorp, *Quodlibeta* I, 1, fol. 3ra-rb. See also Siger of Brabant, *Quaestiones in Tertium de Anima,* Qq. VII-VIII, in Van Steenberghen's summary in *Siger de Brabant: Les*

Oeuvres Inédites, pp. 168-169, where as Keeler notes, Siger teaches that the possible intellect is a mover in relation to man, although he says it is more closely united to us than other movers are to their spheres. In the *De Anima Intellectiva,* q. III (written after the *De Unitate Intellectus* of St. Thomas), Siger rejects a doctrine of the intellect as mover, although he affirms that the intellective soul is separated from the body in existence but united to the body in its operation.

[14] Aristotle, *Met.* VIII, 6, 1045a 8-14, 20-25.

[15] Keeler notes that Aristotle is here treating of the Platonists who, because of their doctrine of ideas, cannot explain the unity of a thing defined to which many notes are at-

as they do in their usual way of defining and speaking, they cannot answer and solve the problem. But if it is as we say: that this indeed is matter, but that is form, and this indeed is in potency, but that is in act, then there will not seem to be any further doubt."

#69. But if you say that Socrates is not one thing simply but one by a conjunction of mover and thing moved, many difficulties follow.

First, since each thing is one in the same way that it is being, it follows that Socrates would not be a being, and that he would not be in a species nor in a genus; and further that he would not have any action, because action belongs only to a being. Wherefore we do not say that the understanding of a sailor is the understanding of this whole which consists of the sailor and the ship, but belongs to the sailor only; and likewise understanding will not be the act of Socrates, but only of the intellect using the body of Socrates. For only in the whole which is something that is one and being, is the act of a part the act of the whole; and if anyone should say otherwise, he would speak incorrectly.

#70. And if you say that in this way the heaven understands through its mover, the assumption is of something more difficult.[16] For it is through the human intellect that we must come to a knowledge of higher intellects, and not conversely. But if it be said that this individual, which is Socrates, is a body animated by a vegetative and sensitive soul, as seems to follow according to those who hold that this man is not constituted in his species through the intellect, but through the sensitive soul ennobled by some illumination from, or union with, the possible intellect, then intellect is not related to Socrates except as a mover to a thing moved. But according to this, the action of the intellect which is understanding could in no way be attributed to Socrates. And this is clear for many reasons.

(#71-79. The argument is drawn from the fact that this man understands.)

#71. First of all, for this reason which the Philosopher gives in Book IX of the *Metaphysics*, that "for those actions for which the result is something other than their exercise, the actuality is in the thing made, as the act of building is in the thing built and that of weaving is in the thing woven; and likewise in other things and in general, motion is in the thing moved. But for those actions for which there is no other product besides the action, the action exists in the

tributed in its definition. See St. Thomas' interpretation of this passage in *Comm. in Met.* VIII, lect. 5, 1758.

[16] That is, says Keeler, the obscure is explained by something more obscure. On the relation of celestial movers to their bodies, see *Sum. Theol.* I, q. 70.

agents, as sight exists in the one seeing, and contemplation in the one contemplating."[17] So therefore, although it be held that the intellect is united to Socrates as a mover, that does not serve to establish that to understand is in Socrates, still less that Socrates understands; since to understand is an action which is in the intellect only.

From this it is also clear that what they say is false, that is, that the intellect is not the act of the body, but the act of understanding itself is [the act of the body.] For the act of understanding cannot belong to anyone for whom it is not the act of the intellect; because there is no act of understanding except in the intellect, as there is no vision except in sight; whence vision can belong only to that whose act is sight.

#72. Secondly, because the proper act of a mover is not attributed to an instrument or to the thing moved; but rather, conversely, the action of the instrument is attributed to the principal mover; for it cannot be said that a saw disposes the work of art; but it can be said that the craftsman saws, and this is the work of the saw. But the proper operation of the intellect itself is to understand; whence even granted that to understand would be an action crossing over to another like to move, it would not follow that to understand would belong to Socrates, if the intellect were united to him only as a mover.

#73. Thirdly, because in those things whose actions cross over to another, the actions are attributed to the movers and the moved in opposite ways. For according to the process of building, the builder is said to build, but the building [is said] to be built. If therefore to understand were an action that crosses over to another, like to move, even then it should not be said that because the intellect is united to him as a mover, therefore Socrates would understand; but rather that the intellect would understand, and Socrates would be understood; or perhaps that the intellect by understanding would move Socrates, and Socrates would be moved.

#74. Yet it sometimes happens that the action of a mover is carried over to the thing moved. For example, a moved thing itself moves from the very fact that it is moved, and a heated thing heats. Therefore someone could say this: that that which is moved by the intellect, which moves by understanding, understands from the very fact that it is moved.

But Aristotle is opposed to this statement in Book II of the *De Anima,* from which we have taken the principle of this argument. For

---

[17] Aristotle, *Met.* IX, 8, 1050a 30-37. See also St. Thomas, *In Met.* IX, lect. 8, 1864. On the three arguments given in #71-73, see *Sum.* *Theol.* I, q. 76, a. 1; *Q.D. de Anima* 2; *In de Anima* III, lect. 7, 690; *De Spir. Creat.* 2; *Comp. Theol.* 85.

when he had said that that by which we first know and are healed is form, that is knowledge and health, he added: "For it seems that the act of the agents is in the recipient or the thing disposed."[18] In explaining this, Themistius says: "For although sometimes there is knowledge and health from others, namely from a teacher and a doctor; yet we have shown before that the act of the agents exists within the recipient or thing disposed, in beings of nature."[19] Therefore it is the meaning of Aristotle, and it is clearly true, that when a moved thing moves and has the action of a mover, there must be within it some act from the mover from which it has this kind of action. And this is the first principle by which it acts. It is its act and form; just as if something is made hot, it heats by reason of the heat that is in it from whatever made it hot.

#75. Suppose it be granted, therefore, that the intellect moves the soul of Socrates either by illuminating or in any other way. That which is left from the impression of the intellect on Socrates is the first principle by which Socrates understands. But that by which Socrates first understands, just as by sense he senses, Aristotle[20] has proved to be potentially all things. For this reason it has no determinate nature except that it is possible; and consequently it is not mingled with body, but is separate. Therefore even if it be granted that there is some separate intellect moving Socrates, yet it still is necessary that that possible intellect of which Aristotle speaks, be in the soul of Socrates, just like that sense by which Socrates senses, that is in potency to all sensibles.

#76. But it might be said that this individual which is Socrates, is neither something composed of the intellect and the animated body, nor is he just an animated body, but he is only an intellect. Now this is the opinion of Plato, who, as Gregory of Nyssa reports, "on account of this difficulty does not intend man to be composed of soul and body, but to be a soul using a body and, as it were, clothed with the body."[21] But Plotinus also, as Macrobius reports, declares that the soul itself is the man, stating it thus: "Therefore, the real man is not the one who is seen, but rather that which rules what is seen. Thus when the animation departs at the animal's death, the body falls widowed from that which rules it and this is what is seen in man as mortal. But the soul, which is the true man, is a stranger to every condition of mortality."[22]

[18] See *De Un. Int.*, #61, and Aristotle, *De Anima* II, 2, 414a 11-12.
[19] Themistius, *op. cit.*, III, p. 109, lines 68-71.
[20] Aristotle, *De Anima* III, 4, 429a 14-29. See *De Un. Int.*, #19-25.
[21] Nemesius of Emessa, *De Natura Hominis*, c. 3 (PG 40, 593). See Plato, *Laws* XII, 959a; Phaedo 79 C. On Gregory of Nyssa and Nemesius, see note 87 to Chapter I.
[22] Macrobius, *Commentarium in Somnium Scipionis*, ed. F. Eyssenhardt (Leipzig: Teubner, 1893), II, 12,

Now this Plotinus, one of the great [commentators], is placed among the commentators of Aristotle, as Simplicius reports in the *Commentary on the Categories*.[23]

#77. Now this opinion does not seem to be very far from the words of Aristotle. For he says in Book IX of the *Ethics* that "it is characteristic of a good man to work out the good and [to do so] for his own sake; for he does so for the sake of the intellective [part] which each one seems to be."[24] Now he does not say this for this reason, that man is only an intellect, but because that which is foremost in man is the intellect. Whence he says in what follows: "just as the state and every other organized whole seems to be principally what is foremost [in it], so also is man."[25] Whence he adds that each man either is this, "that is an intellect, or is principally this."[26] And I think it is in this sense that both Themistius in the words given above,[27] and Plotinus in the words just cited, have said that man is a soul or an intellect.

#78. For it is proved in many ways that man is not only an intellect or only a soul.

First indeed by Gregory of Nyssa himself who, after citing the opinion of Plato, adds: "But this statement contains something difficult or unsolvable. For how can the soul be one with its clothing? For the tunic is not one with the clothed [person].[28]

Secondly, because Aristotle in Book VII of the *Metaphysics* proves that "man and horse and like things" are not only form, "but a certain whole [composed] of matter and form, taken universally; but the singular, for example Socrates, already is from ultimate matter, and likewise in other things."[29] And he proved it in this way: that no part of the body can be defined without some part of the soul. And when the soul withdraws, eye and flesh can be spoken of only equivocally. This would not be if man or Socrates were only an intellect or soul.

lines 9-10; or *Macrobius' Commentary on the Dream of Scipio*, tr. W. H. Stahl (New York: Columbia University Press, 1952). See Plotinus, *Enneads* I, 1 (tr. S. MacKenna. London: Faber & Faber, 1956). Keeler notes that Macrobius gives a very free treatment of the argument of this treatise.

23 Simplicius, Proem., to *In Aristotelis Categorias Commentarium*, ed. C. Kalbfleisch (Berlin, 1907) (Vol. VIII of the *Commentaria in Aristotelem Graeca*), p. 2, line 3. Keeler notes that "Plotinus, one of the great" seems to be a translation of an expression used by Simplicius, and says that Moerbeke's version of this work of Simplicius, made in the year 1266, has "great Plotinus" (Archiv. S. Petri, Cod. H 6, f. 37r). The word "commentators" was not added in these versions.

24 Aristotle, *Nic. Eth.* IX, c. 4, 1166a 15-17.

25 *Ibid.*, c. 8, 1168b 31-33.

26 *Ibid.*, 1169a 2.

27 See *De Un. Int.*, #53.

28 Nemesius of Emessa, *De Nat. Hom.* c. 3 (PG 40, 593).

29 Aristotle, *Met.* VII, 10, 1035b 27-31. See St. Thomas, *Sum. cont. Gent.* II, 57.

Thirdly, it would follow that since the intellect does not move except through the will, as is proved in Book III of the *De Anima*,[30] this would be among the things that are subject to the will, namely, that man would keep his body when he wished and would cast it off when he wished; it is evident that this is obviously false.

#79. So therefore it is clear that the intellect is not united to Socrates only as a mover; and that even if it were, it would not serve to establish that Socrates would understand. Therefore, those who wish to defend this position should either admit that they themselves know nothing and are unfitted to be opponents of other debaters, or they should admit what Aristotle concludes: that that by which we first understand is the species and the form.

(#80-82. Man is placed in a species by the intellect.—On the supposition of the Averroists, the will would also be separate.)

#80. This conclusion can also be reached from the fact that this man is placed in some species.[31] But each thing derives its species from its form. Therefore that by reason of which this man derives his species is his form. But each thing derives its species from that which is the principle of the proper operation of the species. Now the proper operation of man, in so far as he is man, is to understand, for through this he differs from other animals; and therefore in this operation Aristotle places ultimate happiness.[32] But the principle by which we understand is the intellect, as Aristotle says.[33] Therefore it is necessary that it be united to the body as form, not indeed so that the intellective power itself would be the act of some organ, but because it is a power of the soul which is the act of a physical organic body.

#81. Furthermore, according to their position, the principles of moral philosophy would be destroyed; for what is in us would be taken away. For something is not in us except through the will; and this indeed is called voluntary because it is in us.[34] But the will is in the intellect, as is clear from the statement of Aristotle in Book III of the *De Anima*;[35] from the fact that there is intellect and will in separate substances; and also from the fact that it happens through the will that we love or hate something in general, just as we hate robbers as a class, as Aristotle says in his *Rhetoric*.[36]

[30] Aristotle, *De Anima* III, 10, 433a 14-26.

[31] See *Sum. Theol.* I, q. 76, a. 1; *Sum. cont. Gent.* II, 60; II, 73.

[32] Aristotle, *Nic. Eth.* X, c. 7, 1177a 12-17.

[33] Aristotle, *De Anima* III, 4, 429a 23.

And see *De Un. Int.*, #62.

[34] Aristotle, *Nic. Eth.* III, c. 3, 1111a 22-24.

[35] Aristotle, *De Anima* III, 9, 432b 5. See St. Thomas, *Sum. cont. Gent.* II, 60.

[36] Aristotle, *Rhetoric* II, c. 4, 1382a 6.

#82. If, therefore, the intellect does not belong to this man in such a way that it is truly one with him, but is united to him only through phantasms or as a mover, the will will not be in this man, but in the separate intellect.[37] And so this man will not be the master of his act, nor will any act of his be praiseworthy or blameworthy. This is to destroy the principles of moral philosophy.

Since this is absurd and is contrary to human life (for it would not be necessary to take counsel or make laws), it follows that the intellect is united to us in such a way that it and we constitute what is truly one being. This surely can be only in the way in which it has been explained, that is, that the intellect is a power of the soul which is united to us as form. It remains, therefore, that this must be held without any doubt, not on account of the revelation of faith, as they say, but because to deny this is to strive against what is clearly apparent.

(#83-85. Answer is given to one who objects that the intellect thus becomes a material form.)

#83. It is, in fact, not difficult to answer the arguments that they bring against this. For they say that from this position it follows that the intellect would be a material form,[38] and would not be stripped of all natures of sensible things; and that consequently whatever is received in the intellect, will be received individually as in matter, and not universally. And further, if it is a material form, it is not actually intelligible; and so the intellect will not be able to understand itself, which is clearly false; for no material form is actually but only potentially intelligible, but it is made actually intelligible by abstraction.

Now the solution of these difficulties appears from what was said above. For we do not say that the human soul is the form of the body according to its intellective power, which, according to Aristotle's doctrine[39] is not the act of any organ; whence it remains that the soul, as regards its intellective power, is immaterial and receives things immaterially, and understands itself. Wherefore Aristotle expressly says that "the soul is the place of species, not the whole [soul], but the intellect."[40]

#84. But if it be objected against this that a power of the soul cannot be more immaterial or more simple than the soul's essence, the

---

[37] St. Thomas, *Sum. cont. Gent.* II, 60. See also *De Un. Int.*, #89.

[38] Averroes, *In de Anima*, III, comm. 4, pp. 385-386, lines 62-80. See Siger, *Quaestiones in Tertium de Anima*, Q. VII, in Van Steenberghen, *Siger de Brabant: Les Oeuvres Inédites*, p. 168; also Siger, *De Anima Intel-lectiva*, Q. III (written after the *De Un. Int.*) in Mandonnet, *Siger de Brabant et l'Averroisme Latin au XIIIme Siècle*, p. 153.

[39] Aristotle, *De Anima* III, 4, 429a 24-26; 429a 29 - 429b 4.

[40] *Ibid.*, 429a 27-28.

reasoning would proceed soundly if the essence of the human soul were the form of matter in such a way that it would not exist through its own act of existing,[41] but through the act of existing of the composite, as is true of other forms, which of themselves have neither the act of existing nor an operation apart from their union with matter; and on that account they are said to be immersed in matter. But the human soul exists by its own act of existing, in which matter in some way shares [though] not wholly comprising it, since the dignity of this form is greater than the capacity of matter; nothing therefore prevents the soul from having some operation or power that matter cannot reach.

#85. Moreover, let him who says this consider that if this intellective principle, by which we understand, were to exist with an existence that is separate and distinct from the soul which is the form of our body, it would be in itself understanding and understood; and it would not understand at one time and at another not. Furthermore, it would not need to know itself through intelligibles and through acts but through its own essence, like other separate substances. And furthermore, it would not be appropriate for it to need our phantasms for understanding;[42] for it is not found in the order of things that superior substances need inferior substances for their own principal perfections; just as celestial bodies are neither formed nor perfected for their own operations from inferior bodies. Therefore there is great improbability in the statement that the intellect is a kind of principle that is separate according to its substance and yet that it is perfected and comes to know actually through species received from phantasms.

[41] See *De Un Int.*, #27-28.

[42] *Q.D. de Anima* 2; *Sum. cont. Gent.* II, 96-98.

Chapter IV.

(#86-98. The possible intellect is not one for all men.)

(#86-91. If such a unity were posited, there would exist only one being that understands and one that wills.)

#86. Now that we have considered these points concerning their position that the intellect is not the soul which is the form of our body, nor part of the soul, but something separate according to its substance, what remains to be considered is this: that they say that the possible intellect is one in all [men]. Perhaps there might be some reason to say this concerning the agent intellect, and many philosophers have held this.[1] For no difficulty seems to follow, if many things are perfected by one agent, just as by one sun all the visual potencies of animals are perfected for seeing. Yet even this would not be the meaning of Aristotle, who held that the agent intellect is something in the soul, and for this reason he compared it to light.[2] But Plato, holding that there is one separate intellect, compares it to the sun, as Themistius says.[3] For there is but one sun, but many lights diffused by the sun for seeing. But whatever may be the case with the agent intellect, to say that the possible intellect is one for all men seems impossible for many reasons.

#87. First of all, because if the possible intellect is that by which we understand, it must be said that the individual man who understands either is intellect itself or that the intellect formally inheres in him, not indeed in the sense that it would be the form of the body, but because it is a power of the soul which is the form of the body. But if someone should say that the individual man is intellect itself, it follows that this individual man would not be different from that individual man, and that all men would be one man, not indeed by a sharing of the species, but in the sense that there would be only one individual.[4]

If on the other hand, intellect is in us formally, as has already been said, it follows that there would be diverse souls for diverse bodies. For just as man is [composed] of body and soul, so this man, for example Callias or Socrates is [composed] of this body and this soul. But if souls are diverse, and the possible intellect is a power of the soul by which the soul understands, the possible intellect must be different

[1] See St. Thomas, *In Sent.* II, d. 17, q. 2, a. 1; *Q.D. de Anima* 16; *Sum. Theol.* I, q. 79, a. 4; Avicenna, *De Anima* V, 5, fol. 25rb, in Klubertanz, pp. 125-126; Averroes, *In de Anima* III, comm. 19, p. 441, lines 30-33.

[2] Aristotle, *De Anima* III, 5, 430a, 15-16.

[3] Themistius, *op. cit.* VI, p. 235, lines 10-11.

[4] See *Sum. Theol.* I, q. 76, a. 2.

in number. For it is impossible to imagine that in diverse things there be a power that is numerically one.

Now if anyone should say that man understands by the possible intellect as by something that belongs to him, but which is a part of him not as a form but as a mover, it has already been shown above that if this position is held, it can in no way be said that Socrates understands.[5]

#88. But let us grant that Socrates would understand by reason of the fact that the intellect understands, although the intellect be only a mover, as a man sees by reason of the fact that his eye sees. And to follow out the comparison, let it be held that for all men there is an eye that is numerically one; it remains to be asked whether all men would be one who sees or many who see.

To investigate the truth of this, we must consider that the question about the first mover is one thing, and that about the instrument, another.[6] For if many men use numerically one and the same instrument there are said to be many operators; for example, when many use one machine to throw or lift a stone. But if the principal agent be one, using many things for instruments, nevertheless the operator is one, but perhaps the operations are diverse because of the diverse instruments. But sometimes even the operation is one, although many instruments are required for it. Thus, therefore, the unity of the one operating is viewed not according to the instruments, but according to the principal agent using the instruments.

Therefore, in the aforesaid position, if the eye were the principal agent in man, which would use all the powers of the soul and parts of the body as instruments, the many having one eye would be one who sees. But if the eye be not the principal agent in man, but something which uses the eye would be more primary than it, and this would be diverse in diverse men, there would indeed be many seeing but by one eye.

#89. Now it is clear that the intellect is that which is the principal agent in man, and that it uses all the powers of the soul and the members of the body as if they were organs. And on this account Aristotle said subtly that man is intellect "or is principally this."[7] If, therefore, there is one intellect for all, it follows of necessity that there be one who understands and consequently one who wills and one who uses according to the choice of his will all those things by which men are diverse from one another. And from this it further follows that there would be no difference among men in respect to the free choice

[5] See *De Un. Int.*, #79. Also *Sum. Theol.* I, q. 76, a. 2; *Sum. cont. Gent.* II, 73; *Q.D. de Anima* 3.

[6] See *Sum. Theol.* I, q. 76, a. 2.

[7] Aristotle, *Nic. Eth.* IX, c. 8, 1169a 2.

of the will, but it [the choice] would be the same for all, if the intellect in which alone would reside pre-eminence and dominion over the use of all other [powers] is one and undivided in all. This is clearly false and impossible. For it is opposed to what is evident and destroys the whole of moral science and everything which relates to the civil intercourse which is natural to man, as Aristotle says.[8]

#90. Furthermore, if all men understand by one intellect, howsoever it be united to them, whether it be as a form or as a mover, it follows of necessity that at one time and with respect to one intelligible there be numerically one act of understanding for all men. For example, if I understand a stone and you likewise, there will have to be one and the same intellectual operation in me and in you.[9] Because for the same active principle, regardless of whether it be form or mover, and with respect to the same object, the operation of the same species at the same time can be only one in number. This is clear from what the Philosopher says in Book V of the *Physics*.[10] Whence if there were many men having one eye, the act of seeing of all of them would be only one with respect to the same object at the same time.

#91. Similarly, therefore, if the intellect were one in all men, it follows that there would be only one intellectual action for all men understanding the same thing at the same time; especially since none of those things by which men are said to differ from one another would share in the intellectual operation. For the phantasms are preparations for the action of the intellect, as colors are for the act of sight. Therefore the act of the intellect would not be diversified by their diversity, especially in respect to one intelligible. Yet they hold that it is by these phantasms that the knowledge of this man and the knowledge of that man are diverse, in so far as this man understands those things of which he has phantasms, and that man understands other things of which he has phantasms.[11] But in two men who know and understand the same thing, the intellectual operation itself can in no way be diversified by the diversity of the phantasms.

(#92-95. This unity is opposed to the words of the Philosopher concerning the possible intellect and the habit of knowledge.)

#92. But it must still be shown that this position is clearly opposed to what Aristotle says. For when he had said of the possible intellect that it is separate and that it is all things potentially, he adds:

[8] Aristotle, *Pol.* I, 1, 1253a 2-3.
[9] See St. Thomas, *Q.D. de Anima* 3; *De Spir. Creat.* 9.
[10] Aristotle, *Phys.* V, 4, 227b 21 - 228b

1. See also VII, 1, 242a 32 - 242b 4.
[11] See Averroes, *In de Anima* III, comm. 5, p. 400, lines 380-390; p. 412, lines 724-728.

"when it thus becomes singulars (that is in act), as one who knows is said to be such [an agent knowing] actually";[12] that is, in this way: as knowledge is an act, and as one who knows is said to be in act in so far as he has the habit.[13] Then he adds: "This happens when he can without delay act through himself. It indeed is therefore even then in potency in a certain way, yet not in the same way as before learning or discovering."[14] And afterwards, when he had inquired "If the intellect is simple and impassible and has nothing in common with anything else, as Anaxagoras said, how will it understand if to understand is to undergo something?"[15] And to explain this, he answers by saying: "that the intellect is in a certain way potentially the intelligibles, but it is actually nothing before it understands. It must be like a tablet on which nothing is actually written; indeed this is the case with the intellect."[16]

It is therefore Aristotle's position that the possible intellect, before learning or discovering, is in potency, like a tablet on which nothing is actually written. But after learning and discovering, it is in act according to the habit of science, by which it can act through itself, although even then it is in potency to actual consideration.

#93. Here three things must be noted. First, that the habit of science is the first act of the possible intellect itself, which according to this [habit] comes into act and can act through itself. But science is not only according to the illumined phantasms, as some say, nor is it a capability that is acquired by us from frequent meditation and exercise so that we may be in contact with the possible intellect through our phantasms.[17]

Secondly, it should be noted that before our learning or discovering, the possible intellect itself is in potency like a tablet on which nothing is written.

Thirdly, that by our learning or discovering, the possible intellect itself is put into act.

#94. But these [views] can in no way stand, if there be one possible intellect for all who are, who will be, and who have been. For it is clear that the species are retained in the intellect (for it is the place of species, as the Philosopher had said above).[18] And further, knowledge is a permanent habit. If therefore through some previous man, the intellect has been put into act according to some intelligible spe-

[12] Aristotle, *De Anima* III, 4, 429b 5-7.
[13] See *Sum. cont. Gent.* II, 73.
[14] Aristotle, *De Anima* III, 4, 429b 7-9.
[15] *Ibid.*, 429b 23-25.
[16] *Ibid.*, 429b 30 - 430a 2.
[17] See Avicenna, *De Anima* V, 6, fol. 26rb-va, in Klubertanz, pp. 130-132. See also *Sum. cont. Gent.* II, 74; *De Ver.* q. 10, a. 2; *Sum. Theol.* I, q. 79, a. 6.
[18] Aristotle, *De Anima* III, 4, 429a 27-28.

cies, and has been perfected according to the habit of science, that habit and those species remain in it.

But since every recipient must be lacking that which it receives, it is impossible that through my learning or discovering, those species be acquired in the possible intellect.[19] For even if someone should say that through my discovery the possible intellect would be put into act regarding something new, for example, if I discover some intelligible that has been discovered by no previous man; yet this cannot happen in learning; for I can learn only what one who teaches me has known. Therefore it is in vain to say that before learning or discovering, the intellect was in potency.

#95. But someone might add that men always existed, according to the opinion of Aristotle;[20] and that therefore there would not have been a first man understanding; and so through no one's phantasms have the intelligible species been acquired in the possible intellect, but the intelligible species of the possible intellect are eternal.[21] In vain therefore did Aristotle posit the agent intellect, which would make intelligibles in potency to be intelligible in act. In vain, too, did he hold that phantasms are related to the possible intellect as colors are related to sight, if the possible intellect gets nothing from the phantasm.

Besides, it would seem to be very unreasonable that a separate substance should receive from our phantasms and that it would be able to know itself only after our learning or understanding; because Aristotle after the foregoing words adds: "And it can then understand itself,"[22] that is, after learning or discovering. For a separate substance is intelligible in itself; therefore, if the possible intellect were a separate substance, it would understand itself through its own essence. For this it would not need intelligible species that would come to it through our understanding or discovery.

(#96-98. The reply of those who say that Aristotle is speaking of the possible intellect only in so far as it is in contact with us, is not sufficient.)

#96. Now if they should wish to avoid these difficulties by saying that Aristotle made all of the preceding remarks about the possible intellect in so far as it is in contact with us and not in so far as it is in itself,[23] it must first be said that Aristotle's words do not mean this.

[19] St. Thomas, *De Spir. Creat.* 9.
[20] Aristotle, *On Generation and Corruption*, II, 11, 338a 16 - 338b 20; II, 10, 336b 25 - 337a 1; Averroes, *In de Anima* II, comm. 34, pp. 182-183, lines 51-58.

[21] St. Thomas, *Sum. cont. Gent.* II, 73.
[22] Aristotle, *De Anima* III, 4, 429b 9. See *Sum. cont. Gent.* II, 96-98.
[23] Averroes, *In de Anima* III, comm. 5, p. 404, lines 500-510; pp. 411-412, lines 707-710, 724-728.

On the contrary, he speaks of the possible intellect itself according to what is proper to it, and in so far as it is distinguished from the agent intellect. Then if the force of Aristotle's words is ignored, let us hold, as they say, that the possible intellect would have from eternity intelligible species through which it is in contact with us according to the phantasms that are in us.

#97. For the intelligible species which are in the possible intellect and the phantasms which are in us must be related in one of these three ways: One of them is that the intelligible species which are in the possible intellect, are received from the phantasms which are in us, as the words of Aristotle imply; and this cannot be according to the aforesaid position, as was shown.[24] Now the second way is that those species would not be received from phantasms, but would shine upon our phantasms; for example, if there were some species in the eye shining upon the colors which are in the wall. Now the third way is that the intelligible species which are in the possible intellect, would neither be received from phantasms nor would they impress something upon the phantasms.

#98. Now if the second is posited, that is, that the intelligible species illumine the phantasms and for this reason they would be known; it follows, first, that phantasms are made actually intelligible not through the agent intellect, but through the possible intellect according to its own species. Secondly, that such an illumination of the phantasms would not be able to make the phantasms intelligible in act; for phantasms are made intelligible in act only through abstraction; but this would be a reception rather than an abstraction. And further, since every reception is according to the nature of the thing received, the illumination of the intelligible species that are in the possible intellect, will not be in the phantasms that are in us in an intelligible way, but in a sensible and material way. And thus we would not be able to understand the universal through an illumination of this kind. But if the intelligible species of the possible intellect are neither received from phantasms nor shine upon them, they will be entirely unrelated and have no proportion to them; nor would the phantasms contribute anything to understanding. But this is contrary to what is evident.

So therefore in every way it is impossible that there should be only one possible intellect for all men.

---

[24] See *De Un. Int.*, #95.

CHAPTER V.

(#99-124. Solution of the arguments attacking the plurality of the possible intellect.)

(#99-105. Objections 1 and 2: The intellect is an immaterial form; therefore it cannot be multiplied according to the multiplication of bodies. That if it were so multiplied, it would endure as one [intellect] after the destruction of the bodies.)

#99. It now remains to answer those arguments by which they strive to reject the plurality of the possible intellect.

The first of these is: since whatever is multiplied according to the division of matter is a material form, substances that are separate from matter are not many in one species. If, therefore, there were many intellects in many men who are numerically divided from one another by the division of matter, it would follow of necessity that the intellect would be a material form.[1] This is against the words of Aristotle and against the proof by which he proves that the intellect is separate.[2] If, therefore, it is separate and is not a material form, it is in no way multiplied according to the multiplication of bodies.

#100. They rely so much on this argument that they say that God could not make many intellects of one species in different men. For they say that this would imply a contradiction; because to have a nature that may be numerically multiplied is different from the nature of a separate form.[3]

But they go further, being willing to conclude from this that no separate form is one in number nor is it anything individuated. They say that this is apparent from the word itself; because a thing is not one in number unless it is one of a number. But a form freed from matter is not one of a number, because it does not have in itself the cause of number, since the cause of number is from matter.

#101. But to begin with the latter point, they do not seem to know the proper meaning of what was just mentioned. For Aristotle says in

---

[1] Keeler notes that Averroes constantly proceeds on the supposition that if one applies Aristotle's definition, "the first act of the body" to the intellective soul, it must be considered as a material form. See Averroes, *In de Anima* III, comm. 5, p. 402, lines 432-438. See also Siger, *Quaestiones in Tertium de Anima*, Q. IX, in Van Steenberghen, *Siger: Les Oeuvres Inédites*, p. 169; also *De Anima In-* *tellectiva*, VII, in Mandonnet, *op. cit*, p. 165.

[2] Aristotle, *De Anima* I, 1, 403a 10-12; I, 4, 408b 17-18; II, 2, 413b 25-28; III, 5, 430a 18-23. See discussion in *De Un. Int.* #8-9, 25, 31, 36-39.

[3] Siger, *Quaestiones in Tertium de Anima*, Q. IX, in Van Steenberghen, p. 169; *De Anima Intellectiva*, VII, in Mandonnet, p. 166.

Book IV of the *Metaphysics:* "The substance of each thing is one but not accidentally," and that "one is nothing else except being."[4] A separate substance, therefore, if it is being, is one according to its substance, especially since Aristotle says in Book VIII of the *Metaphysics* that those things which do not have matter, do not have a cause [outside themselves] for their being one and for their being.[5] But one, in Book V of the *Metaphysics*, is spoken of in four ways, namely, in number, species, genus, proportion.[6] It should not be said that any separate substance is one only in species or genus, because this is not to be one simply. It remains, therefore, that any separate substance is one in number. But something is not said to be one in number because it is one of a number; for number is not the cause of a thing being one but conversely, because in being numbered, a thing is not divided; for one is that which is not divided.

#102. Further, it is not true to say that every number is caused by matter; for Aristotle would have sought in vain the number of separate substances. Aristotle also holds in Book V of the *Metaphysics* that many is said not only of number but of species and genus.[7]

Nor is it true to say that a separate substance is not singular and something individual; otherwise it would not have any operation since acts belong only to singulars, as the Philosopher says,[8] whence he argues against Plato in Book VII of the *Metaphysics*[9] that if ideas are separate, an idea will not be predicated of many, nor will it be able to be defined, just as is the case with other individuals which are unique in their species, like the sun and the moon. For matter is not the principle of individuation in material things except in so far as matter cannot be participated in by many because it is the first subject not existing in another.[10] Therefore even concerning the idea, Aristotle says that if the idea were separate, it would be something, that is, an individual[11] which could not possibly be predicated of many.

#103. Separate substances, therefore, are individuals and singular. But they are not individuated by matter, but by the very fact that it is not their nature to be in another, and consequently they are not participated in by many.

From this it follows that if it is the nature of some form to be participated in by another in such a way that it is the act of some matter, that [form] can be individuated and multiplied through rela-

[4] Aristotle, *Met.* IV, 2, 1003 a 31-32.
[5] *Ibid.*, VIII, 6, 1045a 36 - b 7.
[6] *Ibid.*, V, 6, 1016b 31-35.
[7] *Ibid.*, 1016b 33 - 1017a 6.
[8] *Ibid.*, I, 1, 981a 16-17.
[9] *Ibid.*, VII, 15, 1040a 8-30.

[10] See *In Sent.* IV, d. 12, q. 1, a. 1, ad 1 and ad 3; *Sum. Theol.* III, q. 77, a. 2.
[11] See St. Thomas, *In Met.* VII, lect. 15, 1612; *Sum. Theol.* I, q. 76, a. 2, ad 3.

tion to matter. But it has already been shown above[12] that the intellect is a power of the soul which is the act of the body. In many bodies, therefore, there are many souls, and in many souls there are many intellectual powers which are called intellects. Nor on this account does it follow that the intellect is a material power, as was shown above.[13]

#104. Now if anyone should object that, if they are multiplied according to bodies, it follows that when the bodies are destroyed, many souls would not remain, the solution is clear from what has been said above. For anything is a being in so far as it is one, as is said in Book IV of the *Metaphysics*.[14] Therefore, just as the to be of the soul is indeed in the body inasmuch as it is the form of the body, nor does it exist before the body, and yet after the body is destroyed it still remains in its to be, so each soul remains in its own unity, and consequently many souls in their manyness.[15]

#105. Now they argue very crudely to show that God could not effect that there be many intellects, since they believe that this would involve a contradiction. For even granted that it were not of the nature of the intellect to be multiplied, it would not need to follow on this account that the multiplication of the intellect would involve a contradiction. For nothing prevents a thing from having from another cause, an effect for which it does not have a cause in its own nature. Just as a heavy thing does not have from its own nature the property of being high up, yet that a heavy thing be high up does not involve a contradiction; but for a heavy thing to be up according to its own nature would involve a contradiction. So therefore if the intellect were naturally one for all men because it would not have a natural cause of multiplication, it could nevertheless receive multiplication from a supernatural cause, and this would not imply a contradiction. This we say not because of the case in question, but rather lest this form of arguing be applied to other topics; for so they might conclude that God could not effect that the dead rise again and that the blind have their sight restored.

(#106-113. Objections 3: The thing understood is one for all; therefore the intellect is also one for all.)

#106. But further, for the defense of their error, they propose another argument. For they ask whether the thing understood is completely one in me and in you, or two in number and one in species. If the thing understood is one, then the intellect will be one. If two in

[12] *De Un. Int.,* #3-82.
[13] *De Un Int.* #38, 83-85.
[14] Aristotle, *Met.* IV, 2, 1003b 30-34.

[15] See *Sum. Theol.* I, q. 76, a. 2, ad 2; *Q.D. de Anima* 3; *De Spir. Creat.* 9, ad 3; *Comp. Theol.* 85.

number and one in species, it follows that the things understood will have an understood object; for whatever are two in number and one in species are one thing [as] understood, because there is one quiddity through which it is understood; and so it would proceed to infinity, but this is impossible.[16] Therefore it is impossible that the things understood should be two in number in me and in you. There is, therefore, only one thing [understood] and the intellect is only one in number for all.

#107. Now it must be asked of those who think that they are so subtle in their argument whether [the fact] that the things that are understood are two in number and one in species is against the notion of the thing understood in so far as it is understood, or in so far as it is understood by man. And it is clear, according to what they hold, that this is against the notion of the thing understood in so far as it is understood. For it is of the notion of the thing understood, in so far as [it is] of this kind, that it have no need of anything being abstracted from it, in order that it may be understood. Therefore, according to their reasoning, we can simply conclude that there is only one thing understood, and not merely one thing understood by all men. And if there is only one thing understood, according to their reasoning it follows that there is only one intellect in the whole world, and not merely in men. Therefore, our intellect is not only a separate substance, but it is even God Himself. And the plurality of separate substances would be totally destroyed.

#108. Now if anyone should wish to answer that the thing understood by one separate substance and the thing understood by another is not one in species, because the intellects differ in species, he would be deceiving himself; because that which is understood is related to understanding and to the intellect, as an object is related to an act and a power. Now the object does not receive species from an act nor from a power, but rather conversely. It must therefore be simply admitted that what is understood of one thing, for example, a stone, is one only, not merely for all men but also for all beings that understand.

#109. But it remains to be asked: what is that thing understood? For if they say that the thing understood is one immaterial species existing in the intellect, it escapes their notice that they are in some way going over to the doctrine of Plato, who held that no knowledge can be derived from sensible things, but all knowledge is from one separate form. For it is irrelevant to the question whether someone should say that the knowledge that is had of a stone is from one separ-

---

[16] See Averroes, *In de Anima* III, comm. 5, p. 411, lines 713-717; St. Thomas, *De Spir. Creat.* 9, ad 6.

ate form of stone or from one form of stone which is in the intellect; for in either case it follows that knowledge is not of things which are here, but only of separated things. But because Plato[17] posited immaterial forms of this kind, subsisting through themselves, he was also able to posit with this many intellects participating in the knowledge of one truth from one separated form. But because they posit immaterial forms of this kind (which they say are things understood) in the intellect, they must hold that there is only one intellect, not merely for all men, but also absolutely.

#110. It must therefore be said according to Aristotle's position, that what is understood, what is one, is the nature itself or quiddity of the thing. For natural science and other sciences are about things, not about understood species. For if the thing understood were not the stone's very nature which is in things, but a species which is in the intellect, it would follow that I would not understand the thing that is the stone, but only the intention which is abstracted from the stone. But it is true that the nature of the stone as it is in singulars, is potentially intelligible but it is made actually intelligible by reason of the fact that species from sensible things, by means of the senses, reach the imagination, and that by the power of the agent intellect, the intelligible species are abstracted, and these exist in the possible intellect. Now these species are not related to the possible intellect as things understood, but as species by which the intellect understands[18] (just as the species which are in vision are not things themselves that are seen, but those by which vision sees), except in so far as the intellect reflects upon itself, and this cannot occur in sense.

#111. Now if to understand were an action that crosses over to external matter, like to burn and to move, it would follow that to understand would be according to the way in which the nature of things has its being in singulars, just as the burning of fire is according to the mode of the burnable. But because to understand is an action that stays within the knower himself, as Aristotle says in Book IX of the *Metaphysics*,[19] it follows that to understand is according to the mode of the knower, that is, according to the requirement of the species by which the knower understands.

Now this [species], since it is abstracted from individuating principles, does not represent the thing according to individual conditions, but only according to a universal nature. For if two things are joined in fact, nothing prevents one of them from being able to be represented without the other even in sense; whence the color of

[17] For Plato's view, see Aristotle, *Met.* I, 6, 987b 4-18.

[18] See *Sum. Theol.* I, q. 85, a. 2.

[19] Aristotle, *Met.* IX, 8, 1050a. 34-36.

honey or of an apple is seen by the sense of sight without the flavor of that thing. Thus, therefore, the intellect understands a universal nature by abstraction from individuating principles.

#112. It is therefore one thing which is understood both by me and by you. But it is understood by me in one way and by you in another, that is, by another intelligible species. And my understanding is one thing, and yours, another; and my intellect is one thing, and yours, another. Whence Aristotle says in the *Categories* that some knowledge is singular with reference to its subject "as a certain grammatical [point] is indeed in a subject, that is, in the soul, but is not said of any subject."[20] Whence also my intellect, when it understands itself to understand, understands a certain singular act; but when it understands "to understand" absolutely, it understands something universal. For singularity is not opposed to intelligibility, but materiality is;[21] whence, since there are some immaterial singular things, as was said above concerning separate substances,[22] nothing prevents singulars of this kind from being understood.

#113. Now from this it is clear in what way there is the same knowledge in the pupil and in the teacher.[23] For it is the same in relation to the thing known, but not, however, in relation to the intelligible species by which each one knows. For in this respect knowledge is individuated in me and in him. The knowledge which is in the pupil need not be caused by the knowledge which is in the teacher as the heat of the water by the heat of fire, but rather as the health which is in the matter [is caused] by the health which is in the soul of the doctor. For just as in a sick man there is a natural principle of health to which the doctor furnishes aids for the achieving of health, so in the pupil there is a natural principle of knowledge, namely the agent intellect and self-evident first principles; now the teacher furnishes certain aids by deducing conclusions from self-evident principles. Whence also the doctor tries to cure in a manner in which nature would cure, namely by heating and chilling; and the teacher leads to knowledge in the same way in which the one who learns would acquire knowledge by himself, namely by proceeding from the known to the unknown. And just as health is achieved in a sick man not according to the power of the doctor, but according to the capability of nature; so also knowledge is caused in the pupil not according to the power of the teacher, but according to the capability of the one learning.

[20] Aristotle, *Categories*, c. 2, 1a 25-27.
[21] *Sum. Theol.* I, q. 76, a.2, ad 3.
[22] See *De Un. Int.*, #102-103.
[23] See Averroes, *In de Anima* III, comm. 5, pp. 411-412, lines 717-721; St. Thomas, *Sum. cont. Gent.* II, 75, ad 3; *Sum. Theol.* I, q. 117, a. 1; *De Spir. Creat.* 9, ad 7; *De Ver.* q. 11, a. 1.

(#114-116. Objection 4: If many intellectual substances were to remain after the destruction of their bodies, they would be inactive.)

#114. But they raise a further objection, that if many intellectual substances would remain after the destruction of their bodies, it would follow that they would be inactive; as Aristotle in Book XI of the *Metaphysics*[24] argues that if there were separate substances not moving a body, they would be inactive.[25] If they were to consider well the text of Aristotle, they could easily resolve this difficulty. For Aristotle, before he proposes this reasoning, says first: "Wherefore it is reasonable to maintain that there are so many substances and immovable principles; for to say it is necessary may be left to more competent thinkers."[26] From this it is clear that he himself is following some probability; he does not impose a necessity.

#115. Further, since what is inactive does not attain the end toward which it tends, it cannot be said even with probability that separate substances would be inactive if they would not move bodies; unless perchance it be said that the movements of bodies are the ends of separate substances. But this is quite impossible, since an end is superior to those things that tend towards the end. Whence Aristotle does not show here that they would be inactive if they did not move bodies, but that "every impassible substance that has in itself attained the best, must be considered an end."[27] For it is the greatest perfection of each thing that it not only be good in itself, but that it cause goodness in others. But it was not clear how separate substances would cause goodness in inferior things, except through the movement of some bodies. This is why Aristotle accepts a kind of probable reason in order to show that some separate substances are manifested only through the movements of the celestial bodies, although this [conclusion] has no necessity, as he himself says.[28]

#116. Now we agree that the human soul does not have the highest perfection of its nature when separated from the body, for the soul is part of human nature. For no part has entire perfection if it is separated from the whole.[29] But it does not, on this account exist in vain; for the end of the human soul is not to move a body, but to understand; and in this is its happiness, as Aristotle proves in Book X of the *Ethics*.[30]

---

[24] Aristotle, *Met.* XII, 8, 1074a 18-22.
[25] Keeler notes that the word "otiosae" is not found in Aristotle, but it does occur in Averroes' commentary on Aristotle's *Met.* XII, c. 8. See 1552 ed., fol. 156b 32.
[26] Aristotle, *Met.* XII, 8, 1074 a 15-17.

See St. Thomas, *Comm. in Met.* XII, lect. 10, 2586.
[27] Aristotle, *Met.* XII, 8, 1074a 17-20.
[28] *Ibid.*, 15-17, and *De Un. Int.*, #114.
[29] See *De Spir. Creat.* 2, ad 5.
[30] Aristotle, *Nic. Eth.* X, c. 7, 1177a 12-18.

(#117-118. Objection 5: The intellects would be infinite in number.)

#117. They object further, in the assertion of their error, that if there were many intellects for many men, then, since the intellect is incorruptible, it would follow that the intellects would be actually infinite according to the position of Aristotle, who held that the world is eternal and that men always existed.[31]

Now Algazel answers this objection in this way in his *Metaphysics;*[32] for he says that "in whatsoever there will have been one of them without the other," quantity or multitude without order, "infinity will not be removed from it, as from the motion of the heavens." And afterwards he adds: "We admit that likewise human souls, which are separable from bodies by death, are infinite in number, although they have their being at the same time, since there is no natural ordering among them upon the removal of which they would cease to be souls, in so far as none of them are causes of the others, but they exist at the same time without any priority or posteriority of nature and position. For priority and posteriority of nature is inconceivable in them unless it be according to the time of their creation. But in their essences, in so far as they are essences, there is no ordering in any way, but they are equal in being; the contrary is true for spaces and bodies, both for a cause and its effect."

#118. But how Aristotle would solve this, we cannot know, because we do not possess that part of the *Metaphysics* in which he wrote about separate substances.[33] For the Philosopher says in Book II of the *Physics,* that "the consideration" of forms "which are separate, yet in matter (in so far as they are separable), is the work of first philosophy."[34] But whatever may be said on this point, it is clear that Catholics, who hold that the world has had a beginning, have no reason for concern.

(#119-121. Objection 6: The unity of the intellect has been asserted by all philosophers except the Latins.)

#119. Now what they [the Averroists] say is clearly false, namely that it was a principle among all philosophers, both Arabs and Peripatetics, though not among the Latins, that the intellect is not multiplied numerically. For Algazel was not a Latin, but an Arab. Avicenna, too, who was an Arab, speaks thus in his book, *On the Soul:* "Prudence and folly and other things of this kind do not exist except in the essence of

---

[31] See St. Thomas, *De Aeternitate Mundi,* near end; Siger of Brabant, *De Anima Intellectiva* VII, Quinto.
[32] Algazel, *Met.* I, tr. 1, div. 6 (p. 40).

See note 9 to Chapter II.
[33] See note 101 to Chapter I.
[34] Aristotle, *Phys.* II, 2, 194b 13-15.

the soul. . . . Therefore, the soul is not one but many in number, and its species is one."[35]

#120. And that we may not omit the Greeks, we should set down on this point the words of Themistius in his *Commentary*. For when he had inquired whether the agent intellect is one or many, he added by way of solution: "Or indeed the first illuminator is one, but those illuminated and illuminating are many. For the sun indeed is one, yet you will say that the light is shared in some way with regard to sight. For on this account, Aristotle did not posit the sun but light in his example, whereas Plato [posited] the sun."[36]

Therefore it is clear from the words of Themistius that the agent intellect, of which Aristotle speaks and which is the illuminator, is not one, and the possible intellect which is illuminated is not one either. But it is true that the principle of illumination is one, that is, some separate substance—either God, according to Catholics,[37] or the last intelligence, according to Avicenna.[38] Now Themistius proves the unity of this separate principle through this that the teacher and the pupil understand the same thing, and this would not be unless the illuminating principle were the same. But it is true that he says afterwards that some had doubted whether the possible intellect is one.[39]

#121. Nor does he say any more on this point, because it was not his intention to touch on the different opinions of the philosophers, but to explain the teachings of Aristotle, Plato, and Theophrastus; whence he concludes: "But what I have said in stating the views of the philosophers on this point is a matter needing extraordinary study and care. It is readily evident, however, that anyone, especially from the texts that we have gathered, will surely receive from them the teaching of Aristotle and Theophrastus, and more so, of Plato himself."[40]

Therefore it is clear that Aristotle, Theophrastus, Themistius, and Plato himself did not hold it as a principle that the possible intellect is one in all [men]. It is also clear that Averroes wrongly reports the opinion of Themistius and Theophrastus concerning the possible and agent intellect. Hence we have for good reason called him the perverter of Peripatetic philosophy.[41] And hence it is astonishing how some, looking only at the commentary of Averroes, presume to state what he himself says: that, with the exception of the Latins, this was the opinion of all the philosophers, both Greek and Arabian.

[35] Avicenna, *De Anima* V, c. 3, fol. 24va, in Klubertanz, p. 121.

[36] Themistius, *op. cit.*, VI, p. 235, lines 7-11.

[37] See St. Thomas, *Sum. Theol.* I, q. 79, a. 4.

[38] Avicenna, *Met.* IX, c. 4, fol. 104v- 105r (Venice, 1508); *De Anima*, V, c. 5, fol. 26rb-va, in Klubertanz, pp. 130-132.

[39] Themistius, *op. cit.*, VI, pp. 235-236, lines 15-40, esp. 30-32.

[40] *Ibid.*, p. 244, lines 2-6.

[41] See *De Un. Int.*, #59.

(#122-123. The opponent puts forth many statements that are rash and unworthy of a Christian man.)

#122. It is deserving of even greater wonder or even of indignation that someone[42] who professes that he is a Christian, should presume to speak so irreverently about the Christian Faith, as when he says that the Latins do not hold this as a principle, that is, that there is only one intellect, because perhaps their law is against it. Here there are two evils: first, because he doubts whether this be against the faith; secondly, because he implies that he is outside this law. And because he later says: this is the reasoning by which Catholics seem to hold their supposition, where he calls a teaching of faith a supposition. What he dares to assert later is no less presumptuous: that God cannot make many intellects, because this would involve a contradiction.

#123. But what he says later is still more serious: "I necessarily conclude through reason that the intellect is one in number; but I firmly hold the opposite through faith."[43] Therefore he thinks that faith is concerned with some propositions whose contraries can be necessarily concluded. But since only a necessary truth can be concluded necessarily, and the opposite of this is something false and impossible, it follows, according to his remark, that faith would be concerned with something false and impossible, that not even God could effect. This the faithful cannot bear to hear.

It is also not without great rashness that he dares to dispute about those things that do not pertain to philosophy but are matters of pure faith, for example, that the soul may suffer hell fire,[44] and that he dares to say that the teachings of the doctors on this point should be rejected. With equal reasoning he could argue about the Trinity, the Incarnation, and other teachings of this kind. In such a way only an ignorant man would speak.

(#124. Conclusion.)

#124. This, therefore, is what we have written to destroy the afore-said error not by means of the teachings of faith, but by means of the

[42] Keeler notes that it is not known for certain who the opponent is whom St. Thomas corrects here and whose words he seems to be citing. It is commonly thought to be Siger, although the words cited here are not found in his works nor in other extant writings of the Averroists. However, in #124, the last section, St. Thomas seems to be criticizing his adversary's oral teaching.

[43] See *De Un. Int.*, #100, 105. Keeler notes that Siger does oppose to faith, the authority of the philosophers and their arguments. These arguments, even where they seem unanswerable, must yield to the faith. See *De Anima Intellectiva* III and VII.

[44] Siger, *Quaestiones in Tertium de Anima*, q. XI, in Van Steenberghen: *Siger: Les Oeuvres Inédites*, p. 170.

arguments and words of the philosophers themselves. But if there be anyone boasting of his knowledge, falsely so-called, who wishes to say something against what we have written here, let him not speak in corners, nor in the presence of boys who do not know how to judge about such difficult matters;[45] but let him write against this treatise if he dares;[46] and he will find not only me who am the least of others, but many other lovers of truth, by whom his error will be opposed or his ignorance remedied.

[45] Keeler notes that it seems to be implied here that the Averroists had already begun to circulate their opinions privately in small gatherings. (See Mandonnet, *op. cit.*, p. 211) That they did this in fact shortly thereafter seems clear from a decree of September 2, 1276. (*Chart. Univ. Paris.* I, p. 539) See Introduction, Part C, note 34.

[46] Keeler notes that in some parts of the *De Anima Intellectiva* (q. III and q. VII) Siger makes references to this writing of St. Thomas. See Introduction, Part C; also Van Steenberghen, *Siger de Brabant . . .*, pp. 551-554.

BOOKS USED IN NOTES TO THE TRANSLATION

Albert, St., *Opera Omnia,* Vol. V. Paris: Vives, 1890.

Alexander of Aphrodisias, *De Intellectu et Intellecto,* in G. Théry, *Alexandre d'Aphrodise.* Kain, Belgium: Le Saulchoir, 1926.

Algazel, *Metaphysica,* ed. J. T. Muckle, *Algazel's Metaphysics.* Toronto: St. Michael's College, 1933.

Aristotle, *De Anima, Metaphysics, Physics, On Generation and Corruption, Categories, Nicomachean Ethics, Rhetoric, Politics, On the Generation of Animals,* in *The Basic Works of Aristotle,* ed. R. McKeon. New York: Random House, 1941.

——. *The Works of Aristotle Translated into English,* 12 vols., ed. W. D. Ross. Oxford: Clarendon Press, 1908-1952.

Augustine, St., *City of God,* in *Basic Writings of Saint Augustine,* Vol. II, ed. W. J. Oates. New York: Random House, 1948.

Averroes, *Commentarium Magnum in Aristotelis de Anima Libros,* ed. F. S. Crawford. Cambridge, Mass.: Mediaeval Academy of America, 1953.

——. *Destructio Destructionum Philosophiae Algazelis,* ed. B. H. Zedler, Milwaukee: Marquette University Press, 1961.

Avicenna, *De Anima.* Venice, 1508. In the transcription of G. P. Klubertanz, S.J. St. Louis: Saint Louis University, 1949.

Baconthorp, John. *Quodlibeta.* Venice, 1527.

Denifle, H. and A. Chatelain, *Chartularium Universitatis Parisiensis,* I. Paris, 1889.

Diels, H., *Die Fragmente der Vorsokratiker.* Berlin: Wedimann, 1937.

Grabmann, M., *Forschungen über die lateinischen Aristoteles übersetzungen des XIII Jahrhunderts, Beiträge zur Geschichte der Philosophie und Theologie des Mittelalters,* XVII, 5-6. Münster, 1916.

Liber de Causis, in O. Bardenhewer, *Die Pseudo-aristotelische Schrift über das reine Gute, bekannt unter den Namen liber de Causis,* Freiburg, 1882.

Macrobius, *Commentarium in Somnium Scipionis,* ed. F. Eyssenhardt. Leipzig: Teubner, 1893.

——. *Commentary on the Dream of Scipio,* tr. W. H. Stahl. New York: Columbia University Press, 1952.

Mandonnet, P., *Siger de Brabant et l'Averroisme Latin au XIIIme Siècle.* Louvain: Institut Supérieur de Philosophie, 1911.

Nemesius of Emessa, *De Natura Hominis,* in Migne, *Patrologiae Cursus Completus, Series Graeca,* Tome 40, 503-818. Paris, 1857-1866.

Pelster, F., *Die Griechisch-lateinischen Metaphysikübersetzungen des Mittelalters. Beiträge zur Geschichte der Philosophie und Theologie des Mittelalters,* Supplementband 11, pp. 89-118 Münster, 1923.

——. "Die Übersetzungen der Aristotelischen Metaphysik in den Werken des hl. Thomas von Aquin," in *Gregorianum* III, 16 (1935), pp. 325-348, 531-561; 17 (1936), pp. 377-406.

Plato, *Dialogues,* 3 vols., tr. B. Jowett. Oxford: Clarendon Press, 1953.

Plotinus, *Enneads,* tr. S. MacKenna. London: Faber and Faber, 1956.

Proclus, *Elements of Theology*, tr. E. R. Dodds. Oxford: Clarendon Press, 1933.

Salman, D., "Saint Thomas et les Traductions Latines des Métaphysiques D'Aristote," *Archives d'Histoire Doctrinale et Littéraire du Moyen Âge*, VII. Paris: Vrin, 1933.

Siger of Brabant, *Quaestiones de Anima Intellectiva*, in P. Mandonnet *Siger de Brabant et l'Averroisme Latin au XIIIme* Siècle, vol. II. Louvain: Institut Supérieur de Philosophie, 1911.

————. *Quaestiones in de Anima III*, in F. Van Steenberghen, *Siger de Brabant*, vol. I. (Les Philosophes Belges, XII). Louvain: Institut Supérieur de Philosophie, 1931.

Simplicius, *In Aristotelis Categorias Commentarium*, ed. C. Kalbfleisch. (*Commentaria in Aristotelem Graeca*, vol. VIII). Berlin, 1907.

Themistius, *Paraphrasis eorum quae de Anima Aristotelis*, in *Thémistius: Commentaire sur le Traité de l'Âme d'Aristote: Traduction de Guillaume de Moerbeke*, ed. G. Verbeke. Louvain: Publications Universitaires de Louvain, 1957.

Thomas Aquinas, St., *Tractatus de Unitate Intellectus contra Averroistas*, ed. L. W. Keeler, S.J. Rome: Gregorian University, 1936, 1946, 1957.

————. *Quaestiones Disputatae de Anima*, in *Quaestiones Disputatae*, Vol. II. Turin, Rome: Marietti, 1949.

————. *The Soul: A Translation of St. Thomas Aquinas' De Anima*, by J. P. Rowan. St. Louis: Herder, 1949.

————. *In Aristotelis Libros de Anima Commentarium*. Turin, Rome: Marietti, 1948.

————. *Aristotle's de Anima with the Commentary of St. Thomas Aquinas*, tr. K. Foster and S. Humphries. New Haven: Yale University Press, 1951.

————. *Quaestiones Disputatae de Spiritualibus Creaturis*, in *Quaestiones Disputatae*, Vol. II. Turin, Rome: Marietti, 1949.

————. *On Spiritual Creatures*, tr. M. C. Fitzpatrick and J. J. Wellmuth. Milwaukee: Marquette University Press, 1949.

————. *Summa Theologiae*, 5 vols. Ottawa, 1941-1945.

————. *Basic Writings of St. Thomas Aquinas*, tr. A. C. Pegis, 2 vols. New York: Random House, 1945.

————. *Summa contra Gentiles*. Rome: Leonine, 1934.

————. *On the Truth of the Catholic Faith*, 4 vols. New York: Doubleday Image Books, 1955-1957.

————. *Scriptum super Libros Sententiarum Magistri Petri Lombardi*, ed. P. Mandonnet. 4 vols. Paris: Lethielleux, 1929-1947.

————. *In Duodecim Libros Metaphysicorum Aristotelis Expositio*. Turin, Rome: Marietti, 1950.

————. *In Octo Libros Physicorum Expositio*. Turin: Leonine, 1954.

————. *In Librum de Sensu et Sensato Commentarium*. Turin, Rome: Marietti, 1949.

————. *De Aeternitate Mundi contra Murmurantes*, in *Opuscula Philosophica*. Turin, Rome: Marietti, 1954.

————. *Quaestiones Quodlibetales*. Turin, Rome: Marietti, 1931.

————. *Quaestiones Disputatae de Veritate*, Vol. I. Turin, Rome: Marietti, 1949.

————. *Truth*. 3 vols. Chicago: Henry Regnery Co., 1952-1954.

————. *Quaestiones Disputatae de Potentia Dei*, Vol. II. Turin, Rome: Marietti, 1949.

————. *On the Power of God.* Westminster, Md.: Newman Press, 1952.

————. *Compendium of Theology,* tr. C. Vollert. St. Louis: Herder, 1949.

Van Steenberghen, F., *Siger dans l'Histoire de l'Aristotélisme,* vol. II of *Siger de Brabant.* (Les Philosophes Belges, Tome XIII) Louvain: Institut Supérieur de Philosophie, 1942.

Zeller, E. *Aristotle and the Earlier Peripatetics,* tr. F. C. Costelloe and J. H. Muirhead. London: Longmans, Green & Co., 1897.

(Note: The references are to the section numbers in the treatise.)

Abstraction: #110-112
Alexander of Aphrodisias: #56
Algazel: #58, 117, 119
Anaxagoras: #20, 22, 92
Arabs: #57-59; 119-121
Aristotle: #1-26; 28-37; 39-50; 53; 60-62; 64; 68; 71; 74-81; 83; 86; 89-90; 92; 94-97; 99; 101-102; 104; 110-112; 114-118; 120-121.
Averroes: #1; 7-8; 23; 56; 59; 63-67; 121.
Averroists: #17
Avicenna: #57; 119; 120

Boethius: #34

Catholics: #118; 120; 122
Commentator: See Averroes

Empedocles: #19

Faith: position of one intellect for all men opposed to, #2; relation to reason, #123-124.
Form of matter and material form: relation and distinction: #28, 30, 37-38, 46, 83-84, 99

God, power of: #100, 105, 122-123
Greeks: #5; 57; 59; 120-121
Gregory of Nyssa: #5; 33; 76; 78

Infinite number: problem of an actual infinite number: #117-118
Intellect, Agent: part of soul: #53; might be some reason for saying it is one: #86
Intellect, Possible: Summary of Averroes' view: #1;
a substance separate in its being from the body: objections: #3-85;
relation to soul, according to Aristotle: #4-5, 7-8, 11-14, 16, 22, 26, 50, 53, 59, 60-82;
not a power in the body: #23, 27;
in what sense it is "separate": #8-9, 16, 25;
has no corporeal organ: #26, 28, 40;
compared with sense: how like sense and how unlike sense: #17-26;
absurd consequences of unity of: #86-91;
not united to body as a mover: #67-79, 88;
objections to plurality of, and answers to objections: #99-123

Knowledge: requirements on part of knower: #19-21;
a transitive or immanent action? #71-74, 111;
as habit: #92-94;
object of: #109-110;
nature of: #111

Latins: #2; 59; 119; 121-122
Life: characteristics of: #6

Macrobius: #76
Matter as principle of individuation: #102-103
Moral order: effect of Averroes' view of intellect on: #81-82, 89

One of a number and one as being: #100-101

Peripatetics: #2; 51; 59; 119
Phantasm: relation to intellect, according to Averroes, and criticism of this view: #63-66, 91, 95-98
Philosopher, The. See Aristotle
Plato: #5; 7; 48; 76; 78; 86; 102; 109; 121
Platonists: #33
Plotinus: #5; 76; 77

Separated spiritual substances: are individuals and singular: #103-104, 112;
question of their finality: #114-116
Simplicius: #76
Soul: Aristotle's definition of: #3, 11, 13;
as substantial form: #3, 10, 25, 30, 38, 62;
if form of body, how incorruptible: #32, 34-35; 37-38;
answers to objections about soul as form: #44-50;
as act of the body: #4-5, 26-28, 50;
powers of: #6, 9, 10-12;
as place of species: #24;
not a mover: #5, 67-70;
question of its knowledge and existence after death: #41, 104
Species, Intelligible: in Averroes' view, and criticism of this view: #63, 65-66, 95-98;
nature of: #110-113

Teaching and learning: #113
Themistius: #39; 51-53; 54; 56; 74; 77; 86; 120; 121
Theophrastus: #54; 55; 64; 121

MEDIAEVAL PHILOSOPHICAL TEXTS IN TRANSLATION

Translation #17: "Geoffrey of Vinsauf: Instruction in the Method and Art of Speaking and Versifying" by Roger P. Parr-Trans.
This text, of one of the most important mediaeval literary theorists, is here for the first time translated into English.

Translation #18: "Liber De Pomo: The Apple, or Aristotle's Death" by Mary F. Rousseau-Trans.
A significant item in the history of mediaeval thought, never previously translated into English from the Latin.

Translation #19: "St. Thomas Aquinas: On the Unity of the Intellect Against the Averroists" by Beatrice H. Zedler-Trans.
This is a polemical treatise that St. Thomas wrote to answer a difficult problem confronting his times.

Translation #20: "The Universal Treatise of Nicholas of Autrecourt" by Leonard L. Kennedy C.S.B., Richard E. Arnold, S.J. and Arthur E. Millward, A.M.
This treatise gives an indication of the deep philosophical skepticism at the University of Paris in the mid-fourteenth century.

Translation #21 "Pseudo-Dionysius Aeropagite: The Divine Names and Mystical Theology" by John D. Jones-Trans.
Among the most important works in the transition from later Greek to Medieval thought.

Translation #22 "Matthew of Vendôme: Ars Versificatoria (The Art of the Versemaker)" by Roger P. Parr-Trans.
The Text of this, the earliest of the major treatises of the *Artest Poetical* is here translated in toto with special emphasis given to maintaining the full nature of the complete original text.

Translation #23 "Suarez on Individuation, Metaphysical Disputation V: Individual Unity and its Principle" by Jorge J.E. Gracia-Trans.
Gracia discusses in masterful detail the main positions on the problem of individuation developed in the Middle Ages and offers his own original view.

Translation #24 Francis Suarez: On the Essence of the Finite Being as Such, on the Existence of That Essence and Their Distinction. by Norman J. Wells-Trans.
From the Latin "De Essentia Entis Ut Tale Est, Et De Illius Esse, Eorumque Distinctione, by Francisco Suarez, S.J. in the 16th Century.

Translation #25 "The Book of Causes (Liber De Causis)" by Dennis Brand-Trans.
One of the central documents in the dossier on Neo-Platonism in the Middle Ages. Translated from the 13th Century Latin.

Translation #26 "Giles of Rome: Errores Philosophorum" by John O. Riedl-Trans.
A previously little-known work that bears new attention due to revived interest in mediaeval studies. Author makes compilation of exact source references of the Errores philosophorum, Aristotelis, Averrois, Avicennae, Algazelis, Alinkdi, Rabbi Moysis, which were contrary to the Christian Faith.

Translation #27 "St. Thomas Aquinas: Questions on the Soul" by James H. Robb-Trans.
The last major text of St. Thomas on Man as Incarnate spirit. In this last of his major texts on what it means to be a human being, St. Thomas develops a new and unique approach to the question. The introduction discusses and summarizes the key themes of St. Thomas' philosophical anthropology.

James H. Robb, Ph.D. is editor of the Mediaeval Philosophical Texts in Translation.

Copies of this translation and the others in the series are obtainable from:
Marquette University Press
Marquette University
Milwaukee, Wisconsin 53233, U.S.A.

Publishers of:

| • Mediaeval Philosophical Texts in Translation | • Père Marquette Theology Lectures | • St. Thomas Aquinas Lectures |